INTRODUCTION TO JUDAISM

Joseph Kalir

Copyright © 1980 by
University Press of America, Inc.
P.O. Box 19101, Washington, D.C. 20036

All rights reserved
Printed in the United States of America
ISBN: 0-8191-0948-7 (Case)
ISBN: 0-8191-0949-7 (Perfect)

Library of Congress Catalog Card Number: 79-6758

To the memory
of my
GRANDFATHER
who taught me,

and

MY PARENTS
who guided me with love
and died as victims of tyranny

Original drawings by Hilda Kalir

FOREWORD

This book shall introduce the reader to Judaism, its religious aspects and its way of life. It is not a book about the Jewish people and their history, it is not a book about Jewish problems or the State of Israel.

It will describe its customs, its rituals, and the many fascinating concepts within it. Before the emancipation, the Jew lived within a Jewish cultural environment and would not have needed this book. He could study about Judaism in the original Hebrew sources. The Jew of today, who does not, and will no longer live behind walls, is in need of a guide in the language he speaks. This book will, therefore, introduce Judaism's basic ideas to the Jew as well as the non-Jew. Judaism is one of mankind's oldest religions. It has made a very important contribution to what we call now the Judeo-Christian Civilization, to two of the world's most important religions, Christianity and Islam. Despite unending persecutions, Judaism is very much alive today. Yet, not much is known, even in the United States, with her significant Jewish population, about some of the finer points of this heritage. This book wants to shed some light on that which is vague, and hopefully eliminate some of the more common doubts or misconceptions. The approach to this material has been open and free, as is the essence of Judaism itself. It wends its way from the Jewish way of life in general, to the Jewish year and its many highlights, both historical and religious, and some of the basic laws and concepts of the religion.

It is thought of as a textbook.

The sources employed throughout this work should prove of interest to the reader who will find that, aside from the Bible, Talmud and Midrash, some lesser known material has been introduced. That could prove of some value. The author has attempted to accompany each chapter with the appropriate traditional source, along with some lesser known finds. For biblical translations THE HOLY SCRIPTURES and THE PROPHETS were generally used. My thanks to the Jewish Publication Society of America, Philadelphia, PA for the courtesy. I chose my own translations for Talmud and Midrash texts and for the Prayerbooks.

My grateful acknowledgement is offered to the Encyclopedia Judaica, the splendid fountain of knowledge for the one who seeks enlightenment. They allowed me to use and locate material concerning the Jewish groups in America.

The so-called Sephardic pronounciation of the Hebrew language, as used in the State of Israel today, has been employed throughout the book. The reader who is less versed in the cited sources out of the talmudic-rabbinic literature may find additional information on the subject in the chapter "The Oral Law."

I am happy to record my indebtedness and thanks to my dear and beloved wife, Hilda Kalir, for her advice in many of the finer points, for her guidance in matters of artistic style, and for her original drawings which so vividly depict and show the objects, better than words. I am deeply appreciative of the many friendly and creative suggestions and constructive criticisms offered to me by my able and gifted daughter Shula. She also gave her time and patience and diligence for technical assistance and counsel.

My gratitude to them is deep and profound.

To all those who have given me moral aid and encouragement - my loving appreciation.

Joseph Kalir

TABLE OF CONTENTS

FOREWORD . . . . page v

THE JEWISH WAY OF LIFE

    The Jewish Year . . . . page 1

    The First Day of the New Month . . . . page 3

    The Sabbath . . . . page 5

    New Year's Day (Rosh Hashanah) . . . . page 11

    The Day of Atonement (Yom Kippur) . . . . page 15

    Passover (Pessach) . . . . page 19

    Festival of Weeks (Shavuot) . . . . page 25

    Festival of the Booths or Tabernacles (Sukkot) . . page 29

    Chanukkah . . . . page 33

    Purim . . . . page 37

    Fast Days . . . . page 39

THE SERVICE IN JUDAISM . . . . page 41

THE JEWISH LIFE

    Circumcision . . . . page 49

    Bar Mitzvah . . . . page 51

    Marriage . . . . page 53

    The Jewish Home . . . . page 57

    Death and Mourning . . . . page 61

TEACHINGS IN JUDAISM . . . . page 63

    God, The Creator of the World . . . . page 67

    God's Revelation . . . . page 71

God as Redeemer and the Messianic Age . . . . page 75
God and Man . . . . page 81
God and Evil . . . . page 85
Remorse and Atonement . . . . page 89
Man and His Fellow Man . . . . page 93
Man and His Home . . . . page 97
The Individual and Society . . . . page 101
Israel, The Chosen People . . . . page 105
The Land of Israel . . . . page 109
The Hebrew Language . . . . page 113

JUDAISM'S MAIN BOOKS . . . . page 115
The Bible . . . . page 117
The Oral Law . . . . page 121
Jewish Philosophy and Mysticism . . . . page 127

MANY SHADES - ONE JUDAISM
Orthodoxy-Traditionalist . . . . page 133
Conservative Judaism . . . . page 137
Reform Judaism . . . . page 141
Chabad--The Lubavitch Chassidim . . . . page 145

BIBLIOGRAPHY . . . . page 151
INDEX . . . . page 155
ABOUT THE AUTHOR . . . . page 167

THE JEWISH WAY OF LIFE

THE JEWISH YEAR

Judaism has created the concept of eternity. God and His creation are eternal, mankind's life is limited. The individual lives only for a short time period, a limited time of eternity. He learned to divide his time into days, weeks, months and years. The Jewish calendar (Luach in Hebrew, meaning: Tablet) has a long development behind it. It obtained its current format from the scholar Hillel II who lived in Tiberias in the middle of the Third Century C.E. It was he who based the calendar on a secure mathematical-astronomical fundament.

Every Jewish day begins with the preceeding evening and lasts from that evening until the following afternoon. Seven days constitute one week. Weekdays do not have Hebrew names but simply are referred to by ordinal numbers. Only the seventh day has a special name: Shabbat, day of rest.

According to the Jewish tradition, the counting of time, i.e. the calendar, does not begin with an historic event but with the creation of the world. The secular year 1980 corresponds to the Jewish year 5740. Yet, no Jew is compelled to believe that the world is 5740 years old. To the enlightened Jew, this reference to the "Beginning of Time" simply serves as a reminder that time itself is a part of eternity.

THE FIRST DAY OF THE NEW MONTH

The Jewish calendar follows the moon cycle. The original concept of month lives already in the Jewish time table. Some months within the Jewish calendar have 29 days and some have 30. The first day of a month is celebrated as Rosh Chodesh - The First Day of the New Month. If the month has 30 days both the last and first days are celebrated as Rosh Chodesh. Twelve months create one year of 354 days, with occasional years of 353 or 355 days, following a specific system.

The new month system was systematically established in the time of the Second Temple in Jerusalem, by the Sanhedrin, the highest court of the land. After listening to reliable witnesses who observed the new moon, the new month was announced by fire signals relayed from mountain to mountain - or by special messenger. At times the announcement did not reach some communities in time, which caused an inability to celebrate that obligatory holiday on the prescribed day. Hence, the doubling of most Biblical holidays, save the Day of Atonement. When the calendar was fixed, the second day of the holidays became meaningless. Nevertheless, it was kept by the Conservative and Orthodox branches of Judaism, outside of Israel. In the state of Israel the second day of a holiday is not celebrated, except for the New Year commemoration of Rosh Hashanah.

The names of the months are of Babylonian origin. Some of them are also mentioned in the Bible. There is: Nissan (March - April [30 days]), Iyar (April - May [29 days]), Sivan (May - June [30 days]), Tammuz (June - July [29 days]), Av (July - August [30 days]), Elul (August - September [29 days]),Tishri (September - October [30 days]), Marcheshvan (October - November [29 or 30] days), Kislev (November - December [29 or 30 days]), Tevet (December - January [29 days]), Shvat (January - February [30 days]), Adar (February - March [29 days]). The year commenced biblically and historically with Nissan due to Israel's emergence as a people in the Sinai Desert during that month. As we know it today, however, the Jewish year begins with the month of Tishri.

The Jewish calendar has another difficulty. It had to find a way to adapt its moon year of 354 days to the sun year of 365 days. Since the Jewish festivals are bound with certain seasons (Passover is a spring festival and Sukkot, the Festival of the Booths or Tabernacles, is a fall festival) the bridge was gapped by adding one whole month to the Jewish calendar,seven times during the course of 19 years. It was added to the month of Adar every third, sixth, eighth, eleventh, fourteenth, seventeenth and nineteenth year. The leap month is called Adar Sheni (Adar Bet), the other Adar, and has 29 days. A leap year has, as a rule, 384 days, but there are also leap years with 383 and 385 days.

THE SABBATH

When the sun sets on Friday afternoon, the Sabbath begins. It is a holiday and a day of rest in the Jewish world for all alike. Yet Sabbath - the word in Hebrew means Day of Rest - is more than a secular day of rest after six weekdays of work. The Jew sanctifies his life through the Sabbath by placing the Lord at its center and by dwelling on the world's divine origin. Man as such is not, alone, the crowning glory of creation. Neither his sovereignty over the earth and its creatures nor his work are the ultimate aim of his destiny. Only with the seventh day, Sabbath, is creation fulfilled when the creator rested from the work of creation, introducing the Sabbath as the ultimate gift to mankind: The undeniable need to stop, take stock, and search one's soul, a sort of divine battery recharge, achieved by physical and mental serenity.

According to tradition the Sabbath can only be observed by two: God and man. Restless work robs life of its true meaning. The surest path to accomplishment is by finding this divine rhythm of work and rest.

In the ancient Jewish tradition, Sabbath became the day of social equality. Being familiar with the misery of slavery from their old Egyptian days, the Jews gave their Sabbath the freedom to free one and all into the line of direct communication with the self and the divine presence. It is a freedom beyond freedom, which by its existence ennobles the week's work, and with it carves out a space for man in that illusive time called eternity. The traditional Jew expressed the presence of a special soul on that day, the Sabbath Soul, with which the Jew feels each week at one with his maker.

The beauty of the Sabbath lies in the Sabbath itself. The Jewish home is prepared for the festival by the lighting of the Sabbath candles on Friday evening by the matriarch, who sanctifies this beginning with a blessing. The meal, on this evening starts with Kiddush - sanctification of the wine - a prayer which is sung by the patriarch over a cup of wine. Then the Challah - two loaves of white bread - is broken. The Sabbath meals are family oriented, augmented by songs, holiday foods and grace after meals, introduced by Psalm 126.

Sabbath is the second holiest festival in Judaism. It is a day of abstention from any task. Ideally, some of it is to be spent in prayer and some in study. When three stars appear in the sky in the early evening of Sabbath, the day of rest has come to an end. It is marked by a festival ceremony, the Havdalah - sep-

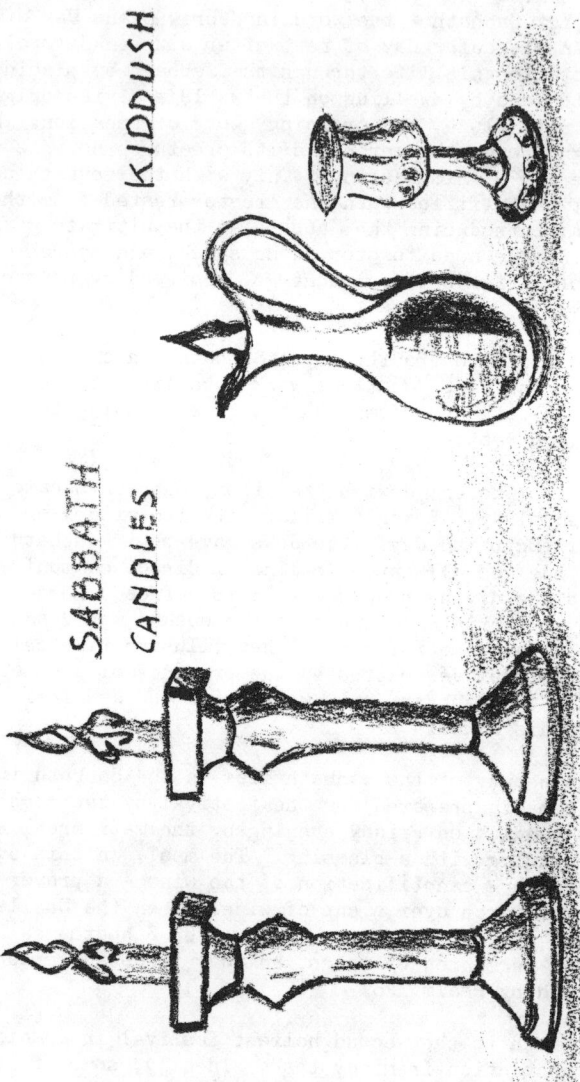

aration - namely the separation between the holy and the secular, Sabbath and the workday. The Havdalah consists of a blessing over a cup of wine, and a blessing over murr and spices which are contained in a silver box. (The spices shall reintroduce to the Jew the workday soul after the Sabbath soul left). And, finally, a blessing over a special candle, thanking God for the gift of light. The Jew who really celebrates the Sabbath as a complete day of rest is to be considered a complete Jew. "More than Israel saved the Sabbath, the Sabbath saved Israel," said a modern Jewish thinker, known under the name of Achad Haam.

> And the heaven and the earth were finished, and all the host of them. And on the seventh day God finished His work which He had made; and He rested on the seventh day from all His work which He had made. And God blessed the seventh day, and hallowed it because that in it He rested from all His work which God in creating had made.
>
> Genesis, 2:1-3

> Remember the Sabbath day, to keep it holy. Six days shalt though labor, and do all thy work. But the seventh day is a Sabbath unto the Lord thy God, in it thou shalt not do any manner of work, thou, nor thy son, nor thy daughter, nor thy man-servant, nor thy maidservant, nor thy cattle, nor thy stranger that is within thy gates. For in six days the Lord made heaven and earth, the sea and all that in them is, and rested on the seventh day; wherefore the Lord blessed the Sabbath day, and hallowed it.
>
> Exodus, 20:8-11

> Six days thou shalt do thy work, but on the seventh day thou shalt rest, that thine ox and thine ass may have rest, and the son of thy handmaid, and the stranger, may be refreshed.
>
> Exodus, 23:12

> The children of Israel shall keep the Sabbath to observe the Sabbath throughout their generations, for a perpetual covenant. It is a sign between Me and the children of Israel forever; for in six days the Lord made heaven and earth, and on the seventh day He ceased from work and rested.
>
> Exodus, 31:16-17

> If you refrain from trampling the sabbath, from pursuing your affairs on My holy day; if you call the sabbath "delight", the Lord's holy day "honored"; and if you

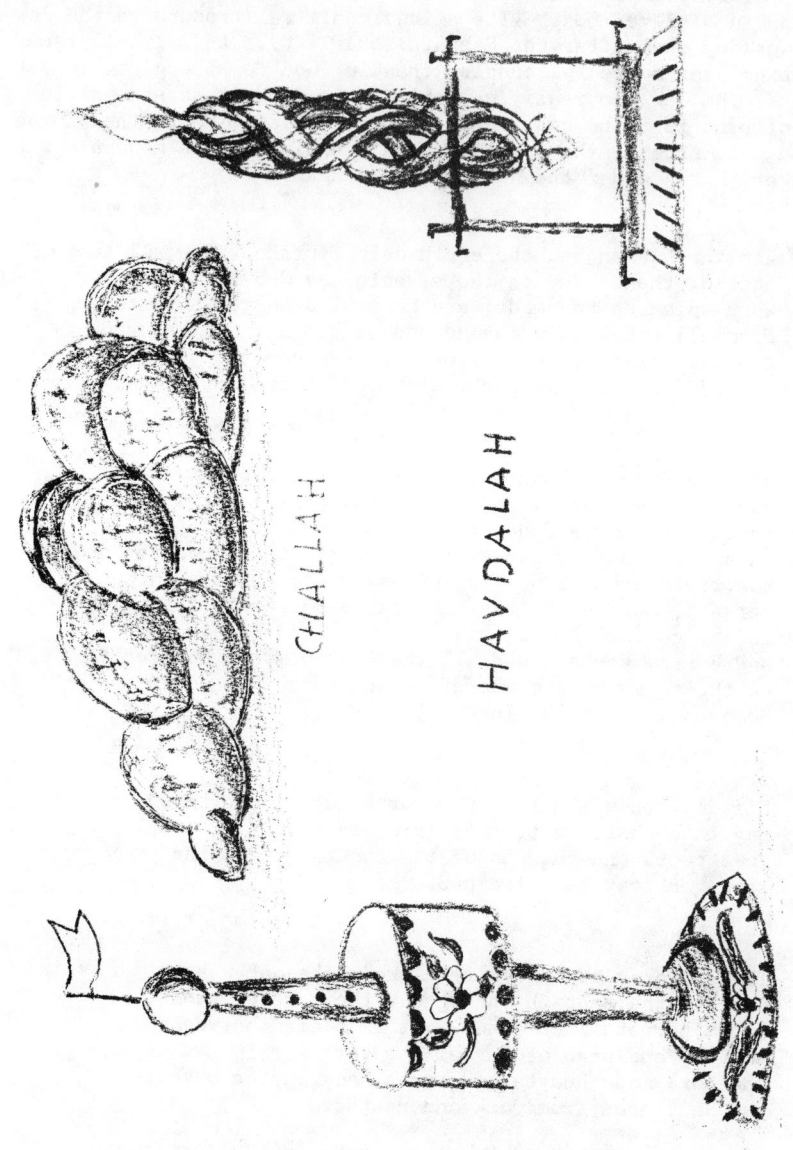

honor it and go not your ways nor look to your affairs, nor strike bargains then you can seek the favor of the Lord. I will set you astride the heights of the earth, and let you enjoy the heritage of your Father Jacob - for the mouth of the Lord has spoken.

                              Isaiah, 58:13-14

And new moon after new moon, And sabbath after sabbath, All flesh shall come to worship Me - said the Lord.

                              Isaiah, 66:23

Rabbi Shimon ben Lakish said: The Holy One gives a special soul to man on Sabbath and at day's end He takes it back.

                              Bab. Talmud Shabbat, 16A

Rabbi Jochanan said on behalf of Rabbi Shimon Bar Jochai: If Israel would observe two Shabbats according to their laws it would be redeemed.

                              Bab. Talmud Shabbat, 118B

Once the Roman emperor said to Rabbi Joshua ben Chananja: How come that your Shabbat meals smell so good? He answered: We have a spice called Shabbat, that we put into our meals, hence, that delectable smell. It works only for those who keep the Shabbat. For those who do not believe in the Shabbat, it does not work.

                              Bab. Talmud Shabbat, 119A

Said Abbajeh: Jerusalem was destroyed because its people did not observe the Shabbat.

                              Bab. Talmud Shabbat, 119B

The Shabbat is one sixth of the hereafter.

                              Midrash Bereshit Rabba, 57

NEW YEAR'S DAY
(Rosh Hashanah)
1 and 2 Tishri

With Rosh Hashanah begins the Jewish New Year and the Yamin Noraim, (the Days of Awe), the traditional name for the New Year's Days and the Day of Atonement. The ten days between the New Year's Days and the Day of Atonement are called Asseret Yemey Teshuva, the Ten Days of **Penitence,** and they are dedicated to prayer, doing penance and good deeds. The Yamin Noraim find the worship services in the synagogue far more heavily populated, and are more intensely observed and participated in, than any other holiday. Prayer becomes an experience, both communal and personal, leading to extensive soul searching on the New Year and the ultimate soul cleansing on the Day of Atonement. Its drawing power is strong enough to compel even the least religious to the House of God.

These holidays have no historical connection as so many other festivals do. The center of these "Days of Awe" is the human being whom God created. It is a time for humankind to seclude itself with thoughts and feelings about his fellow man and about his maker. With the beginning of each New Year, man will approach his creator, newly created, in purity and innocence, marked in the synagogue by the predominance of the color white. The worshipper finds himself in the presence of a white robed rabbi and cantor, an ark containing white mantled Torah scrolls and a brilliant white curtain adorning the ark itself.

Additionally, the New Year's Day is called Yom Teruah, the Day of the Blowing of the Horn, or Yom Hazikaron, the Day of Remembrance, or Yom Hadin, the Day of Reckoning. The first name refers to the most impressive part of the worship service, the blowing of the Shofar. The Shofar is a ram's horn, surely one of man's most primitive musical instruments, with its strange, plantive tones, coming from mankind's ancient times. It was used as the means of calling the population to assembly for important occasions, as we discover as early as the momentuous Ten Commandment scene at Mt. Sinai. It heralded the presence of God and the laying down of the basic ethical axioms of society.

The Shofar is blown twice during New Year's Day service, first shortly after the Torah reading and secondly during the Mussaf prayer (the additional prayer). It is the ultimate communication, the culmination of a whole month (preceding the New Year's Day) of daily Shofar blowings during the Shacharit (morning) service, calling the individual to ready himself during that month (the month of Elul) by means of purification of the soul for the great encounter of the Days of Awe.

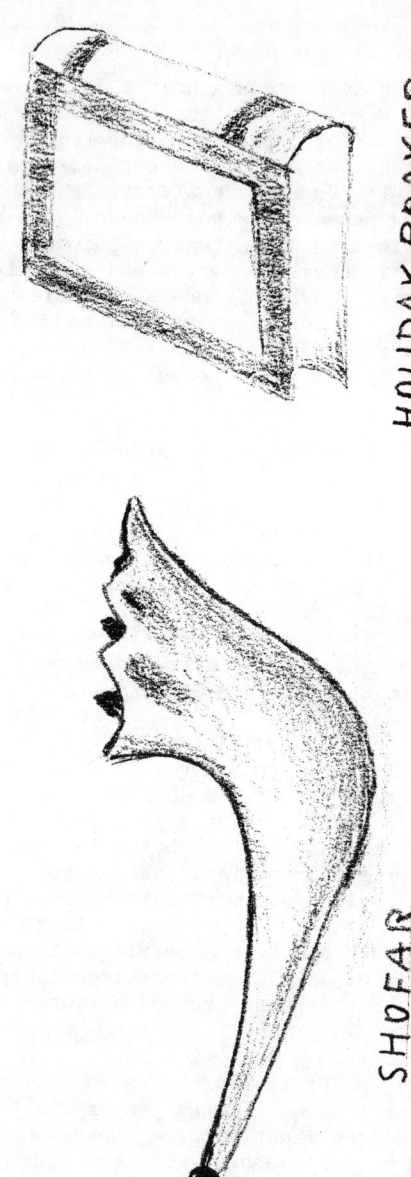

The references Day of Remembrance and Day of Reckoning are often found together. They express the remembrance of the creation of the world and its call to a reckoning before its creator's divine court. As the Jew stands before his judge assessing himself as a member of the community and as an individual and a Jew, he holds the key to resolve his own fate through his prayer and honest intentions. The question of future direction is an oft repeated theme on this day. Will man's resolve result in success or failure, joy or pain? Man himself can be the master of his own destiny.

The Mussaf prayer, (the additional prayer), which is the longest prayer in the Jewish liturgy, is essentially divided into three parts: Malchuyot - God's Kingdom, Zichronot - God's Remembrance, and Shofarot - The Ram's Horns. In Malchuyot, God's omnipresence and splendor are celebrated extensively. Redemption will come when mankind and God will be one, we in serene brotherhood and He in compassionate sovereignty. Zichronot points to God's omnipotence. The prayer attempts to remind the Creator of the covenant He made with humanity, with Noah, with the patriarchs and with the people of Israel so as to allow His judgment and disposition to be lenient. Shofarot reenacts the scene of the revelation at Sinai and the blowing of the ram's horn on that momentous occasion. The same tones will be heard when the world's redemption will be at hand. The strange sound, thus, will be the sound of the ultimate joy.

On the New Year's Days Jews greet each other with the wish: Leshanah Tovah Tikatevu, may you be inscribed for a good new year.

> And the Lord spoke unto Moses saying: In the seventh month, in the first day of the month, shall be a solemn rest unto you, a memorial proclaimed with the blast of horns, a holy convocation.
> Leviticus, 23:23-24

> When a ram's horn is sounded in a town, do the people not take alarm? Can misfortune come to a town if the Lord has not caused it?
> Amos, 3:6

> On the first of Tishri a new year is started.
> Mishnah Rosh Hashanah, 1:1

> Rabbi Jehuda said: On New Year's Day mankind is standing before the divine court and on the Day of Atonement the verdict is sealed.
> Rabbi Kruspedai said in the name of Rabbi Jochanan:

Three books are lying open on New Year's Day: The book
of righteous men, the book of wicked men and the book
of those in between. The righteous are inscribed and
sealed to life, the wicked are inscribed and sealed
to die. The undecided remain between the two from
New Year's Day to the Day of Atonement. If they pass
the test they are inscribed to life, if not, to death.

                        Bab. Talmud Rosh Hashanah, 16A

When somebody goes to the courtroom, he in most cases
wears a dark garment because he does not know how the
verdict will be. Israel on the New Year's Day wears
white garments, eats and drinks and is stirred with
the anticipation that God through His love will judge
kindly.

                        Jer. Talmud Rosh Hashanah, 1:3

THE DAY OF ATONEMENT
(Yom Kippur)
10 Tishri

Yom Kippur, the Day of Atonement, is the crown of the Jewish year. In the Talmud this day is simply called "The Day." It is the time when a Jew devotes his mind and heart solely to prayer. From sundown to sunset he searches his own soul and strives for its renewal and rebirth, so as to fulfill its divine promise.

One of the most important features of this day is the total fast which it commands. It starts, as always, on the evening prior to the day and lasts until the following sunset. Only children and the seriously ill are exempt. From the ages of 13 for a boy and 12 for a girl, Jews choose to exercise this commandment in order to express their readiness to merge with the divine will. All work is forbidden on this highest holiday of Judaism. By subjecting himself to the discomforts of total fast, the Jew achieves total concentration on the meaning and purpose of the day. That is the way to forgiveness and redemption.

It is a directness between man and his maker: No interceding, no middleman. Man stands bare, yet strong and hopeful. It is, for the Jew, the great homecoming. This strict fasting serves, incidently, as an additional reminder of the equality of man before God. All man-made social structures are as naught before Him. The rich and powerful fast in supplication alongside the poor and the needy. Their day in the divine court is neither more comfortable nor easier than their less fortunate brethren. No riches are recognized other than those of love and compassion and no poverty other than their lack. It is an eye opener to those who lose sight of the true concept of equality. It also further illustrates man's mastery over his own destiny. He is born pure, may go awry, but the correction thereof is in his own hands.

One of the interesting concepts found in the liturgy of this day, is the duality of the transgressions enumerated here. Man has transgressed as an individual, but also as a member of his community. The "We" is as important as the "I" (in the prayers of Yom Kippur), and in man's responsibility to his fellow man achieves prime importance on this day.

Another important concept is the Hebrew expression for repentance. It is "Teshuvah" and clearly comes from the root "Shuv" - to return. Hence, further indication that the state of mental purity, of oneness with the divine ethic is the home, the origin, from which man occasionally errs.

Along with the aforementioned unique qualities of this monumental day, there are some additional differences to further emphasize the holiday's singular place, such as the use of the Tallit, the prayer shawl, during the evening service. (Male Jews use the Tallit during the whole year solely for the morning service). The world renown prayer "Kol Nidre" - "All the Vows" - is chanted by the cantor three times. Its stirring melody has so moved its listeners over the years that a classical piece by Max Bruch (a German composer) for cello and orchestra is based on it, bears its name and is part of the standard concert repertoire.

The entire evening has come to be called "Kol Nidre" eve. It is a very ancient prayer which became especially meaningful in Spain in the days of the Marranos (a term used to denigrate the New Christians - converts from Judaism) of Spain and Portugal in the 15th century. These forced converts accepted the new faith solely to win the right to survive, not to find a new religious conviction. And so with "Kol Nidre" they, too, were resolved of the forced vows made during the previous year. As the words state: Kol Nidre...all personal vows, oaths, etc. that a Jew made unwittingly, rashly or unknowingly and that, consequently, cannot be fulfilled during the year (including those made under duress and without free will) should be considered null and void. A strange declaration with which to start a holiday, but it, too, strives to stress the wish and resolve to return to a clean state. Hence, the emphasis of a solemn threefold "Kol Nidre."

Thus, the Jew begins the holiest day of the year - the Sabbat of Sabbats, as it is also called.

At day's end the Neila Service - The locking of the gate - is spoken, summarizing the essence of the day. The concluding sound of the Shofar announces the end of the final service. The day in court is done. The gate is gently locked. Man is embarking on his new journey.

> On the tenth day of this seventh month is the day of atonement. There shall be a holy convocation unto you, and ye shall afflict your souls. And ye shall bring an offering made by fire unto the Lord. And ye shall do no manner of work in that same day. For it is a day of atonement, to make atonement for you before the Lord your God. For whatsoever soul it be that shall not be afflicted in that same day, he shall be cut off from his people. And whatsoever soul it be that does any manner of work in that same day, that soul will I destroy from among his people. Ye shall do no manner of work. It is a statute for ever throughout your generations in all your dwellings. It shall be unto you a sabbath of solemn rest, and ye shall afflict your souls, in the ninth day of

the month at even, from even unto even, shall ye keep your sabbath.

Leviticus, 23:27-32

Cry with full throat, without restraint; Raise your voice like a ram's horn! Declare to my people their transgression, to the House of Jacob their sin. To be sure, they seek Me daily, eager to learn My ways. Like a nation that does what is right, that has not abandoned the Laws of its God, they ask Me for the right way, they are eager for the nearness of God. "Why, when we fasted, did You not see? When we starved our bodies, did You pay no heed?" Because on your fast day you see to your business and oppress all your laborers! Because you fast in the strife and contention, and you strike with a wicked fist! Your fasting today is not such as to make your voice heard on high. Is such the fast I desire a day for men to starve their bodies? Is it bowing the head like a bulrush and lying in sackcloth and ashes? Do you call that a fast, a day when the Lord is favorable? No, this is the fast I desire: To unlock the fetters of wickedness, and untie the cords of the yoke, to let the oppressed go free; to break off every yoke. It is to share your bread with the hungry, and to take the wretched poor into your home; when you see the naked, to clothe him, and not to ignore your own kin. Then shall your light burst through like the dawn and your healing spring up quickly; your vindicator shall march before you, the presence of the Lord shall be your rear guard.

Isaiah, 58:1-8

If the sick one says he needs food on Yom Kippur, one shall listen to him and give it to him.

Bab. Talmud Yomah, 83A

If there would be no Yom Kippur, the world could not exist.

Pirkei Rabbi Eliezer, 46

PASSOVER
(Pessach)
15-22 Nissan

Pessach, as Passover is called in Hebrew, or Chag Hamatzot, the Festival of the Unleavened Bread, along with the Festival of the Weeks and the Festival of the Tabernacles constitute the circle of the three Pilgrimage Festivals. This name was given to them to describe the three annual pilgrimages to Jerusalem required from each Jew. Originally these were nature and harvest festivals which later on received some religious-historic-national overtones. Pessach is Judaism's Freedon Festival in which the deliverance from the Egyptian bondage is celebrated. It is observed for eight days (although Israel and the Reform movement observe seven days) in the spring. The first two days and the last two days are holy days requiring no work and participation in prayer services (in Israel only the first and seventh day, likewise in the Reform movement). At the center of this week are so-called "Half Holidays." The entire Passover week strictly forbids the partaking of any bread or any leavened grain in any form. Hence, the preparation for Passover has always served as the perfect opportunity for spring cleaning. All traces of crumbs and grains are removed, and the home, too, gets a new lease on life.

During the holiday, Matzah, the Unleavened Bread, is eaten. Matzah, the Bread of Affliction, serves as a constant reminder of the poverty suffered by the Israelites in Egyptian bondage, both physically and in social standing. It is the bread baked when finally abandoning Egypt in great haste, needing to forego leavening time.

The big event of the Passover Festival is the Seder celebration in the Jewish home. Seder, which means "order" is celebrated on the two first nights of Passover (in Israel and with the Reform movement only the first night). The Seder receives its name due to the procedural timetable and order followed by the participants. Aside from the esthetic effort put into the physical accoutrements of the evening, the participants will be asked to sip wine at least four times (at prescribed times), as the cups are refilled, and to participate in the service as found in the "Haggadah" provided for all. It is a small book (its name means: The Tale) containing the story of the deliverance from Egyptian bondage, and assorted songs. The Haggadah is one of the most popular books of the Jews. At the Seder it is a chance to accentuate the festive atmosphere and to increase the happy involvement of all family members, primarily the young. This folklore-like book has no known author and consequently no precise time of origin. Theories are that it began during the time of the Mishnah, though it is more likely the result of folklore evolutions of several origins.

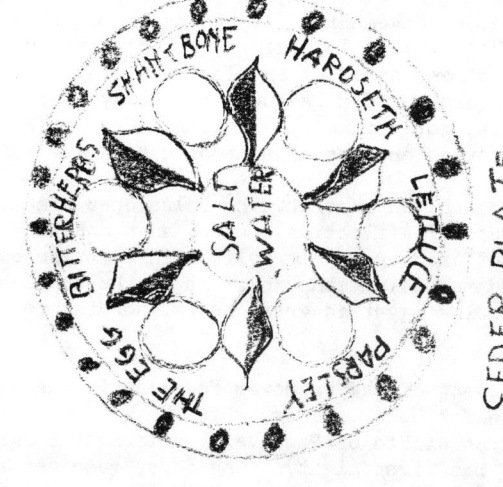

The Seder, the Order, follows the following precise procedures:

1. The Kiddush, the Sanctification of the wine, performed by the head of the household.
2. The washing of hands by the head of the household.
3. The dipping of the greens in the saltwater and eating of some.
4. The breaking in half of the middle Matzah, thus creating the Affikoman (the official dessert).
5. The asking of the "Four Questions" by the youngest participant.
6. The answer to these questions, as provided by the Haggadah, read by the head of the household and the participants.
7. A second washing of the hands, now done by all, in preparation of the festive meal.
8. The first taste of the Passover Matzah.
9. The symbolic bitter herbs (symbolizing those bitter years of bondage) are eaten.
10. The "Hillel Sandwich" of Matzah and bitter herbs is eaten.
11. The elaborate holiday meal is eaten.
12. The hidden Affikoman is eaten after a playful search by the children (the one who finds it gets an award).
13. Grace after the meal.
14. The singing of Passover and assorted freedom songs.

Many an item found on the Seder table bears significant meaning referring to the historical and/or spiritual events of the Egyptian period. Analyzing the Seder plate, placed at the head of the table, we find the previously mentioned Bitter Herbs, the Roasted Egg, going back to the daily sacrifice at the Temple in Jerusalem, the Greens, symbolizing spring, the Charosset (chopped apples, nuts, cinnamon and wine), symbolizing the mortar used by the Israeli slaves in the building tasks, the Shankbone, symbolizing the Paschal lamb, the Saltwater which is a keen and realistic reminder of the tears of humiliation and defeat, shed by the enslaved people for 400 years.

The above items have also been known to be hors d'oevres created by the Romans in their hay day. They, incidently, contributed another detail to this celebration, namely that of the "reclined sitting." That is created primarily for the head of the household who, by reclining, shows the mode of sitting used by Free

Romans. One of the mystical moments of the evening is provided by the filled wine cup left on the table for Eliah, the prophet. His expiration, as told in the Bible, is so strange and inconclusive, that he has been given, in the legend, the task of announcing the messianic era when it arrives. Every Passover he symbolically enters every home and partakes of the wine in a spiritually moving moment of door opening. At this festive moment it is this great, unforgotten prophet who symbolizes the hope of the coming redemption.

Pessach, thus, is in Judaism, the holiday of Freedom, all Freedoms - physical, spiritual, religious, political and emotional. However, we realize annually how many of these freedoms have yet to be achieved.

> Speak ye unto the congregation of Israel, saying: In the tenth day of this month they shall take to them every man a lamb, according to their Fathers' houses, a lamb for a household. And if the household be too little for a lamb, then shall he and his neighbor next unto his house take one according to the number of the souls. According to every man's eating ye shall make your count for the lamb. Your lamb shall be without blemish, a male of the first year. Ye shall take it from the sheep, or from the goats.
>
> Exodus, 12:3-5

> Then Moses called for all the elders of Israel, and said unto them: Draw out and take your lambs according to your families, and kill the passover lamb.
>
> Exodus, 12:21

> And he called for Moses and Aaron by night, and said: Rise up, get you forth from among my people, both ye and the children of Israel. And go, serve the Lord, as ye have said. Take both your flocks and your herds, as ye have said and begone. And bless me also. And the Egyptians were urgent upon the people, to send them out of the land in haste. For they said: We are all dead men.
>
> Exodus, 12:31-33

> And it came to pass at the end of four hundred and thirty years, even the selfsame day it came to pass that all the hosts of the Lord went out from the Land of Egypt. It was a night of watching unto the Lord for bringing them out from the land of Egypt. This same night is a night of watching unto the Lord for

all the children of Israel throughout their generations.

> Exodus, 12:41-42

Three times thou shalt keep a feast unto Me in the year. The feast of unleavened bread shalt thou keep. Seven days thou shalt eat unleavened bread as I commanded thee, at the time appointed, in the month Aviv - for in it thou camest out from Egypt. And none shall appear before Me empty. And the feast of harvest, the first-fruits of thy labours, which thou sowest in the field. And the feast of ingathering, at the end of the year, when thou gatherest in thy labours out of the field. Three times in the year all thy males shall appear before the Lord God.

> Exodus, 23:14-17

The feast of unleavened bread shalt thou keep. Seven days thou shalt eat unleavened bread, as I commanded thee, at the time appointed in the month Aviv, for in the month Aviv thou camest out from Egypt.

> Exodus, 34:18

Encamped at Gilgal, in the steppes of Jericho, the Israelites offered the passover sacrifice on the fourteenth day of the month, toward evening. On the day after the passover offering, on that very day, they ate the produce of the country, unleavened bread and parched grain.

> Joshuah, 5:10-11

The king commanded all the people, "Offer the passover sacrifice to the Lord your God as prescribed in this scroll of the covenant." Now, the passover sacrifice had not been offered in that manner in the days of the chieftains who ruled Israel or during the days of the kings of Israel and the kings of Judah. Only in the eighteenth year of King Josiah was such a passover sacrifice offered in that manner to the Lord in Jerusalem.

> Second Kings, 23:21-23

Because of the good deeds of the women our forefathers were delivered from Egypt.

> Bab. Talmuc Sotah, 11B

Rabbi Jochanan said: At the moment that the Egyptians drowned in the Reed Sea, the angels wanted to sing a song for the Holy One, blessed be He.

But the Holy One, blessed be He told them: When creatures, whom I have created drown in the sea, you will sing a song before Me?!! No!!

> Bab. Talmud Megillah, 10B

Rabbi Levi said: It is the custom of servants to eat standing up. But on the Seder evening one eats sitting to remind you that they were delivered from bondage to freedom.

> Jer. Talmud Pessachim, 10:1

Why do we drink four cups of wine on Passover evening? Rabbi Jochanan said in Rabbi Banaja's name: according to the four expressions for the deliverance "Tell to the children of Israel: I am the Lord and I will bring you out from under the burdens of the Egyptians, and I will deliver you from their bondage, and I will redeem you with an outstretched arm and with great judgments, and I will take you to Me for a people, and I will be to you a God."

> Jer. Talmud Pessachim, 10:1

One day, when Moses, our teacher, watched over the flock of Jethro near the desert, one lamb ran away. He went after it until he caught it. Coming back he found a well and the lamb wanted to drink there. When Moses saw this he said: I did not know that you went away because you were thirsty and now you must be tired. Whereupon he took the lamb on his shoulder and went. Said the Holy One: You have compassion when you watch a flock of sheep so carefully. Now you shall watch and guide my flock: Israel.

> Midrash Shemot Rabba, 2

The children of Israel went out of Egypt full packed with gold and silver which they had taken from the Egyptians. Yet Moses carried another load on his shoulders: a box with Joseph's bones.

> Midrash Devarim Rabba, 11

FESTIVAL OF WEEKS
(Shavuot)
6 (and 7) Sivan

The second of the three Pilgrimage Festivals, called in the Torah Chag Hashavuot, Festival of Weeks, was originally not bound by a special date. Instead, seven weeks were counted from the first day of Passover, leading up to the 50th day on which it was celebrated. This count is traditionally done even today, culminating, as in ancient days, in Shavuot, the Feast of Weeks. The period is called the counting of the Omer - Sefirat Haomer, Omer being a measure of wheat. It dramatizes the ancient tradition of bringing the first wheat harvest to the Temple on Passover day, spending the following 49 days of counting in hopeful prayer to achieve a good harvest. These days have taken on some traditional characteristics of mourning such as no weddings (and for the orthodox: no shaving) to remember the killer plague which hit the ranks of Rabbi Akiba's disciples during the Roman time. The plague miraculously halted on the 33rd day of the counting. It has come to be the traditional "oasis" day in the somber days of Omer counting, when weddings are performed and merriment is permitted. The day is called Lag Ba'omer, using the numerical value of the Hebrew letter constituting the number 33.

As in most Jewish holidays, some of the customs are geared to encourage the participation of the young. Lag Ba'omer carries on this concept in the commemoration of the heroics of Rabbi Shimon Bar Yochai who chose to go into hiding when the Romans forbade the teaching of Torah. Tradition has it that on Lag Ba'omer many of his young students would go to the forest in which he was hiding with bows and arrows and hunting gear in order to mislead any Roman legions as to their intentions. There they had a day's worth of Torah and wisdom imparted to them by the master.

Today, Lag Ba'omer is widely celebrated as "Teacher's Day" in Jewish circles with most students concentrating on outdoor activities. It is said that Rabbi Shimon Bar Yochai died on Lag Ba'omer day and hence his grave in Meron, Israel has been visited by many of his admirers on that day.

The Festival of Weeks has two main characteristics. As a nature holiday, it is the Festival of the First Fruit Harvest, brought in a festive procession to the Temple. As a religious/ spiritual holiday it is the Festival of God's revelation of the Ten Commandments at Mount Sinai. For this festival the synagogues are decorated with leaves and flowers signifying nature's new blossoming. It is a custom among Jews to eat dairy products on this holiday. Shavuot is celebrated two days by the Conservatives and Orthodox Jews outside of Israel (one day only by Reform Jews) and one day in Israel, according to Biblical commandment. In the

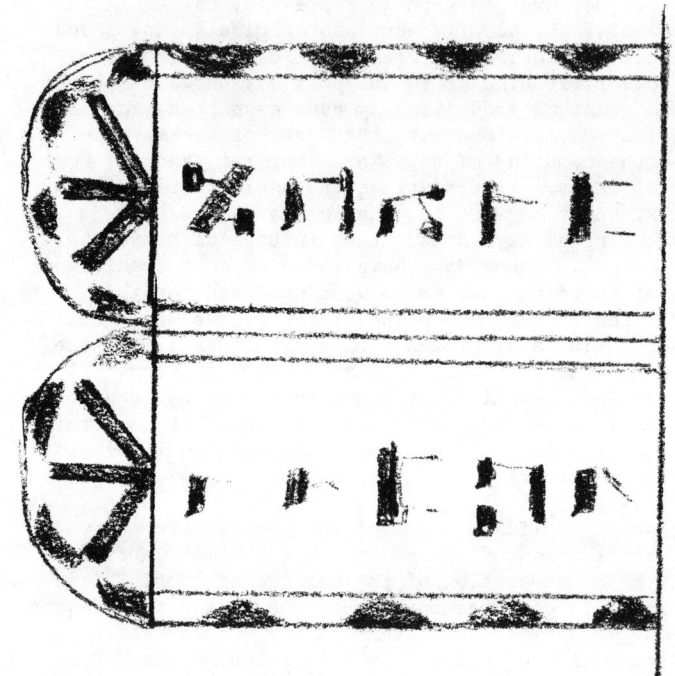

SHAVUOT
FESTIVAL OF THE TEN COMMANDMENTS

Reform and Conservative movements confirmation and graduation
ceremonies of religious schools take place on Shavuot, obviously
as a celebration of the voluntary acceptance of the Ten Commandments by the Jews.

> In the third month after the children of Israel were
> gone forth out of the land of Egypt, the same day came
> they into the wilderness of Sinai. And when they were
> departed from Rephidim and were come to the wilderness
> of Sinai, they encamped in the wilderness. And there
> Israel encamped before the mount. And Moses went up
> unto God, and the Lord called unto him out of the
> mountain, saying: Thus shalt thou say to the house of
> Jacob, and tell the children of Israel: Ye have seen
> what I did unto the Egyptians, and how I bore you on
> eagles wings, and brought you unto Myself. Now therefore, if ye will harken unto My voice, and keep My
> covenant, then ye shall be Mine own treasure from among
> all peoples. For all the earth is Mine. And ye shall
> be unto Me a kingdom of priests, and a holy nation.
> These are the words which thou shalt speak unto the
> children of Israel.
>
> Exodus, 19:1-6

> The choicest first-fruits of thy land thou shalt bring
> into the house of the Lord thy God. Thou shalt not seethe
> a kid in its mother's milk.
>
> Exodus, 23:19

> And ye shall count unto you from the morrow after the
> day of rest (Sabbat) from the day that ye brought the
> sheaf of the waving. Seven weeks shall there be complete.
> Even unto the morrow after the seventh week shall ye
> number fifty days. And ye shall present a new meal-
> offering unto the Lord.
>
> Leviticus, 23:15-16

> And it shall be, when thou comest in unto the land which
> the Lord thy God gives thee for an inheritance, and do
> possess it, and dwell therein. That thou shalt take
> of the first of all the fruit of the ground, which thou
> shalt bring in from thy land that the Lord thy God
> gives thee. And thou shalt put it in a basket, and shalt
> go unto the place which the Lord thy God shall choose
> to cause His name to dwell there. And thou shalt come
> unto the priest that shall be in those days, and say
> unto him: I profess this day unto the Lord thy God,
> that I am come unto the land which the Lord swore

unto our Fathers to give us. And the priest shall take the basket out of thy hand, and set it down before the altar of the Lord thy God.

Deuteronomy, 26:1-4

How were the First Fruits brought to Jerusalem? All the inhabitants of the places which belonged to a district, congregated in the district's capital and stayed there overnight. In the morning the elder spoke to them and said: Come, let us go up to Zion to the Lord's, our God's, house. Those who lived near Jerusalem had fresh figs and raisins. One man went in front of them with a ram's horn and a wreath of olive branches on his head. A man with a flute also marched in front, until they got to Jerusalem. As soon as they arrived there, they sent a messenger to the temple and all decorated their sacrifices. Priests and even Levites came out to meet them. When they walked through Jerusalem the people of the city greeted them with the words: Brethren, men of this and this place, welcome to Jerusalem.

The flute again went in front until they came to the Temple Mount. Here, everybody, including King Agrippa, took his basket on his shoulder and went uphill. As soon as they got there, the Levites started to sing: "I will extol Thee, O Lord, for Thou hast raised me, and hast not suffered mine enemies to rejoice over me." (Psalms, 30:2).

Thereupon whatever was in the basket was sacrificed and what was left in his hands was given to the priests.

Mishna Bikkurim, 3:2-5

Our sages taught: On the sixth of Sivan the Ten Commandments were given to Israel.

Bab. Talmud Shabbat, 86B

FESTIVAL OF THE BOOTHS [OR TABERNACLES]
(Sukkot)
15-23 Tishri

A few days after New Year's days and the Day of Atonement, Jews celebrate the joyful Festival of the Booths, Sukkot, which is the third of the Pilgrimage Festivals. This holiday lasts for seven days, the first two of which are full holidays requiring rest and prayer and the avoidance of work (in Israel and with the Reform movement it is only the first day). The other days are "half" holidays. There are two symbols which are most strongly identified with this holiday: The booth or tabernacle, **Sukkah**, and the Lulav, the festive palm branch. A citrus-like fruit, called Etrog, which grows in Israel, is another symbol of this festival. The Biblical commandment to live in a booth for seven days, requires the Jews to remember their wandering in the wilderness and their forefathers' need to dwell in booths during their wanderings, albeit under divine protection. The historical-agricultural tradition which requires this participation is a tribute to the Hebrew farmer of yore who during the days of the Temple, stayed in these specially built huts in order to more efficiently tend to his fields and vineyards at early morning hours. In its general tenor it is a holiday of thanksgiving for God's generosity.

The building instructions are rather specific: The Tabernacle shall not have a solid roof. It is to be covered with tree branches loosely laid across, so as to allow the moon and the stars to shine through. The booth is decorated with fruits, flowers and other decorations.

The last day of Sukkot is the time in which the farmer concentrated in his prayers on the need for rain. On that day a fervent plea for rain is uttered, lending that day a somewhat serious note. Throughout the festival (except on Sabbath) the Lulav and Etrog, the two symbols of the holiday, are held when the prayer of the psalms (Hallel) is recited and paraded around the synagogue with a Torah scroll leading the way. For the procession the Lulav is shaken as part of this ceremony in a gesture both reminiscent of the wind bringing the rain, and God's presence in all four corners of the world. The Lulav consists of one palm branch, three myrtle branches and two willow branches. All these are symbols of rain. On the seventh day, the Lulav, some willow and myrtle branches are taken on the festival procession with the Torah scroll, for the purpose of reciting specific prayers set aside for this occasion, called "Hoshanah", referring to the word with which they begin. This word which means "Save, Please!" thus gives the seventh day its appellation: "Hoshanah Rabba" - The Great Hoshana's Day. Jewish mysticism gave this day, and especially the night, to Hoshanah Rabba new meaning. From approximately the mid-

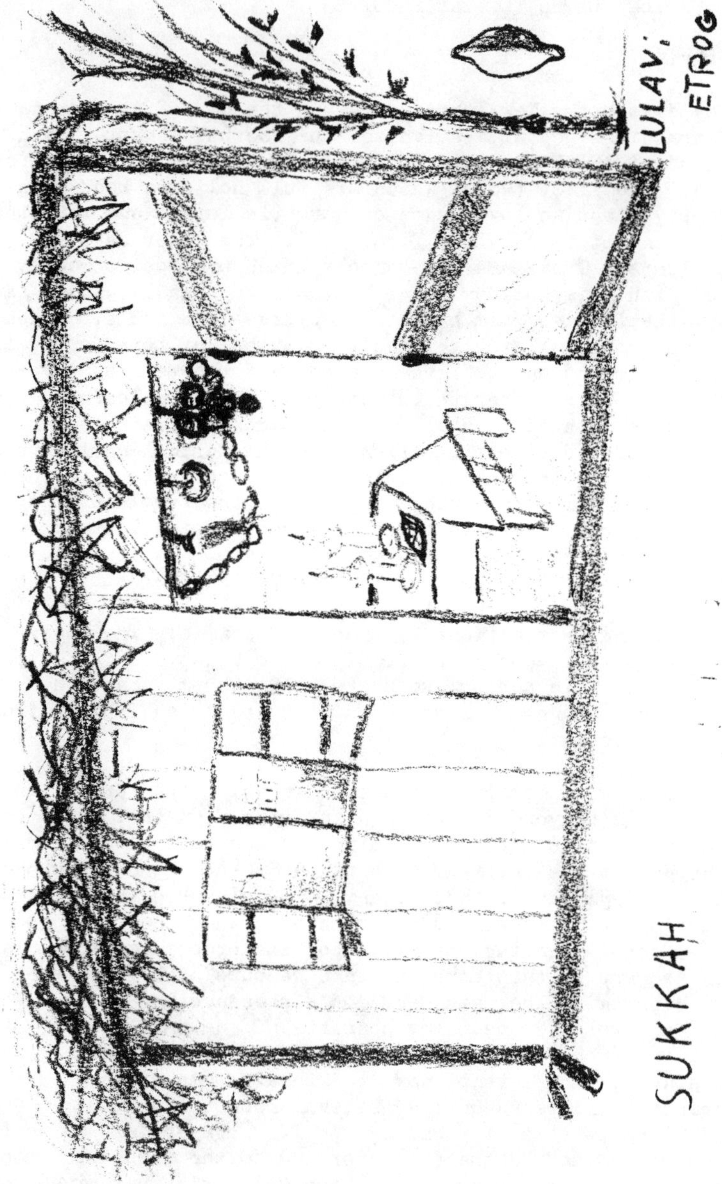
LULAV;
ETROG
SUKKAH

dle of 1500 A.D. it became a custom among mystics to stay up this night reading the Pentateuch, the Psalms and mystic literature. The day takes on a solemn and somber tone, a kind of Day of Atonement, in which the lot of human beings in the coming year is finally sealed. The cantor is dressed in white, the prayers are recited with the melodies of the Day of Atonement and with the Sephardic Jews the Shofar is blown after each of the seven processions.

The eighth day which concludes the Festival of Tabernacles is called Shmini Atzeret, the concluding festival. The Lulav and Etrog are no longer used, yet the **Sukkah** is still there. In the additional prayer (Mussaf) of this day, the festive prayer for rain is recited: "Thou art the Lord our God who causest the wind to blow and the rain to descend for a blessing and not for a curse, for life and not for death, for plenty and not for famine."

Approximately 1,000 years ago, in the Diaspora, the second day of the concluding festival (i.e., the day following Shmini Atzeret) became a special celebration of the Torah, called Simchat Torah. On this day the yearly cycle of the reading of portions of the Torah on Sabbaths and Festivals is concluded, and commences anew with the tradition of calling members of the congregations to the pulpit for reading these weekly portions. These readings take on a special honor. The one called for the concluding paragraph of Deuteronomy is called "Chatan Torah" - The Groom of the Torah. The one who is called for the opening paragraph of Genesis is called "Chatan Bereshit" - The Groom of the Beginning. On the evening and morning of this holiday all the Torah scrolls are taken out of the ark and carried around the synagogue in a procession in which the young are encouraged to participate, waving banners of Biblical themes, and partaking of sweets, expressing the "Joy of the Torah." Hence, the day's name "Simchat Torah." It, too, is a day of thanksgiving for the giving of The Book to mankind.

In Israel (and with the Reform movement) the concluding Festival and the Torah Feast are celebrated on one and the same day.

> On the fifteenth day of the seventh month, when ye have gathered in the fruits of the land, ye shall keep the Feast of the Lord seven days. On the first day shall be a solemn rest, and on the eighth day shall be a solemn rest. And ye shall take out on the first day the fruit of goodly trees, branches of palm-trees, and willows of the brook, and ye shall rejoice before the Lord your God seven days. And ye shall keep it a feast unto the Lord seven days in the year. It is a statute for ever in your generations. Ye shall keep it in the seventh month. Ye shall dwell in

booths seven days. All that are homeborn in Israel shall dwell in booths. That your generations may know that I made the children of Israel to dwell in booths, when I brought them out of the land of Egypt. I am the Lord your God.

> Leviticus, 23:39-43

At the Festival of Booths the amount of rain for the year is decided.

> Mishna Rosh Hashanah, 1:2

During all the seven days one shall have his booth as his dwelling place.

> Mishna Sukka, 2:9

Near Jerusalem, there was a place called Motza. There people went down to collect willows. The willow branches were laid down at the side of the altar so that the heads were hanging over the altar. They blew a long, a short and a long Shofar tune. Everyday they walked round the altar and sang:

"We beseech Thee, O Lord, save now!

We beseech Thee, O Lord, make us now to prosper."

> Mishna Sukka, 4:5

Rabbi Elazar ben Zadok tells: That was the custom in Jerusalem: When somebody left his house or went to the synagogue, he recited "Hear, O Israel" or other prayers and he had his Lulav in his hand. When he read from the Torah or had to raise his hands for the priestly benediction, he put it down on the spot. When he went to visit sick ones or to comfort mourners he took his Lulav in his hand. When he went to school to study he sent it home with his son, his servant or a messenger. Take note, how eager they were to fulfill the commandment.

> Bab. Talmud Sukka, 41B

Our sages taught: It is the duty of everybody to treat his family and his friends with joy on the holidays. As it is said: "And thou shalt rejoice in thy feast, thou, and thy son and thy daughter, and thy man-servant, and thy maid-servant, and the Levite, and the stranger and the Fatherless and the widow, that are within thy gates." (Deuteronomy, 16:14)

> Bab. Talmud Pessachim, 109A

CHANUKKAH
eight days from the 25th of Kislev

The Festival of the Lights or the Festival of the Rededication of the Temple - Chanukkah - is considered one of the minor holidays in Judaism. Work is allowed on these days and the events themselves do not have a biblical-historical origin. It is a relatively young holiday, celebrated as a commemoration of the victories of the Maccabees, or Hasmoneans, over the Syrian king Antiochus Epiphanes, who ruled over Palestine and wanted to force the Jewish people to give up their religion and their holy Temple. Judah Maccabee's (Maccabee means "Hammer") victory in this, the first recorded war for religious freedom, and the rededication of the Temple in the year 164 B.C.E. led to a Jewish independent state. Talmudic legend has it that with the cleansing of the Temple they found a small vessel of pure oil which could be used for ritual purposes in the candelabra (Menorah). There was only enough oil for one day's use, but through a miracle it lasted for eight. Hence, the eight day long celebration observed, both at home and the synagogue which includes a nightly candle lighting ceremony on an escalating scale from one to eight, as the holiday progresses. The candelabra used for this occasion is called "Chanukkiah" rather than the usual "Menorah", clearly bearing the festival's name. With that ceremony the victorious outcome of the battle of this later version of David against Goliath is emphasized in benediction and song. The light with which the other Chanukkah lights are kindled, is called Shamash, servant. With each kindling ceremony, a song from the middle ages called Maoz Tzur - Rock of Strength (or Rock of Ages) - which recalls the deliverance of Israel from similar dangers, is sung.

Although Chanukkah often falls during the Christmas season, it has no relationship to the Christian festival.

The history of Chanukkah is recorded in the two first Maccabean books. They are not Biblical books, but belong to the Apocrypha. They are written in Greek, although the First Maccabean book was written in Hebrew. That original has disappeared. In Talmudic literature, Chanukkah is very seldom mentioned.

Chanukkah is the Festival of the Jewish child. Jewish tradition knows a special Chanukkah game called Dreidel, a four cornered spinning top with Hebrew letters which is played by the young.

And the angel who talked with me came back and woke me as a man is wakened from sleep. He said to me, "What do you see?" And I answered, "I see a lampstand,

CHANUKKIAH

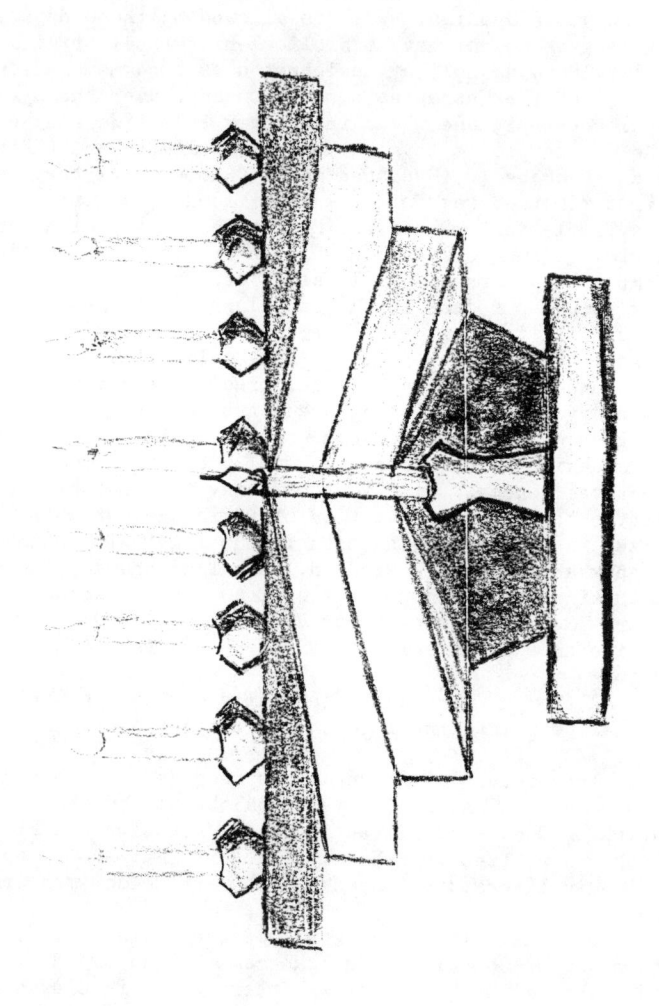

all of gold, with a bowl above it. The lamps on
it are seven in number and the lamps above it have
seven pipes, and by it are two olive trees, one on
the right of the bowl and one on its left." I, in
turn, asked the angel who talked with me, "What
do those things mean, my Lord." "Do you not know
what those things mean?" asked the angel who talked
with me; and I said, "No, my Lord." Then he explained
to me as follows: "This is the word of the Lord to
Zerubbabel: 'Not by might, nor by power, but by
My spirit -- said the Lord of Hosts.'"

Zecharia, 4:1-6

(From the prophetic portion read on the Sabbath of Chanukkah).

What is Chanukkah?

The Rabbis taught: On the 25th of Kislev the Chanukkah
Festivals days start. These are eight days and one
shall not keep any mourning time during these and
shall not fast. When the Syrians penetrated the
Temple they spoiled all the oil that was there. When
the Hasmoneans were victorious and the Syrians were
defeated, the Hasmoneans found, after a long search,
only one small vessel with oil which had the high
priests stamp on it. The oil was enough for one day.
There was a miracle and the oil burned for eight days.
In the following year they pronounced these eight days
as holidays with hymns and thanksgiving songs.

Bab. Talmud Shabbat, 21A

Why do we kindle lights on Chanukkah? When the sons
of the Hasmoneans were victorious over the Syrian
kingdom they entered the Temple and found there
eight wicks of thread. Then they kindled light to
them.

Pesikta Rabbati, 2

GRAGGER NOISE MAKER

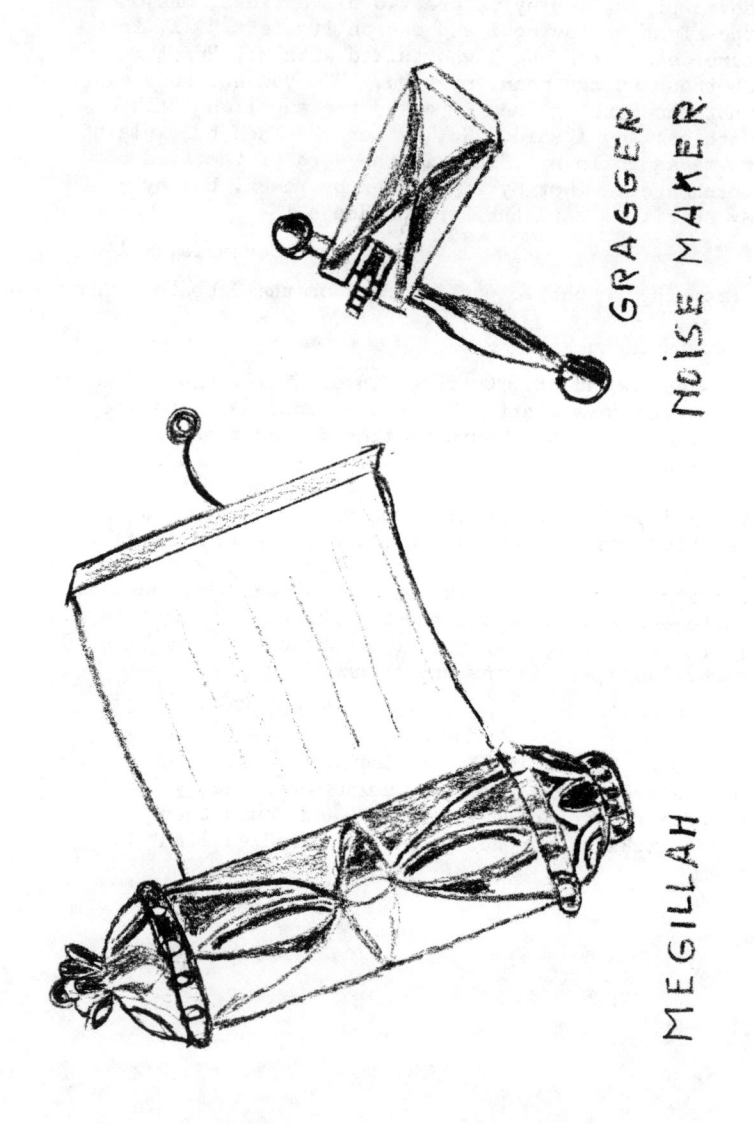

MEGILLAH

PURIM
14 Adar

Purim, as Chanukkah, is a remembrance to the deliverance from great danger. The Book of Esther tells of the plot to which the Persian Jews were subjected by the king's minister Haman. Yet, through Mordechai and his cousin Esther, whom the king had made his wife, they were ultimately spared. Haman drew lots, the singular of which the Book of Esther calls "pur", and thus fixed the day for the destruction of the Jews. The holiday took its name from that "pur", hence "Purim" (i.e., lots). It celebrates benevolence overcoming hatred. On Purim eve and the following morning the story is read in the synagogue from the Book of Esther. This is the main feature of this minor holiday on which work is permitted. It is customary that, during the reading of the Book of Esther - also called the Megillah - the children make a loud noise with rattles (called Gragger) whenever the name of Haman, the arch enemy, is read. In cities which in ancient times were surrounded by a wall (i.e., Jerusalem among others) the additional holiday Shushan Purim is celebrated, named after the Persian capital of Shushan, on the 15th of Adar. Elsewhere, Purim is celebrated on the 14th of Adar. In a Jewish leap year on the 14th of Adar Bet.

On Purim one gives gifts to the poor and to friends. These presents are called Mishloach Manot, the sending of gifts, an expression used in the Book of Esther. Purim is a very joyful minor festival. There is a festive meal eaten, topped by the special pastry which is called Hamantaschen, or Ozney Haman (Haman's Ears).

Purim gave its name to local days of thanksgiving for being saved from danger, in various parts of the world. The Jews in Cairo celebrate, for example, a local Purim as a remembrance of a prevented persecution 400 years ago, and in Frankfurt, Germany there is a "Winz-Purim" which originated in the beginning of 1600 when the antisemitic Winz Fettmilch wanted to destroy the ghetto of the city.

Two Sabbaths before Purim and two Sabbaths after Purim, special portions are read from the Torah. These relate partly to Purim, partly to Pessach. Sabbath "Shekalim" tells of the Shekel donation, which in Biblical times was made before Passover for reparations of the Temple. Sabbath "Zachor" ("Remember") reminds the congregation of Amalek, Israel's arch enemy, allegedly Haman's own ancestors. Sabbath "Para" (cow) contains the passages which describe the cleansing water through which the unclean are cleansed before Pessach. And the Sabbath "Ha-Chodesh" (month) tells, again, about the deliverance from Egypt.

Wherefore they called these days Purim, after the name
of pur. Therefore because of all the words of this
letter, and of that which they had seen concerning
this matter, and that which had come unto them. The
Jews ordained, and took upon them, and upon their
seed, and upon all such as joined themselves unto
them, so as it should not fail, that they would keep
these two days according to the writing thereof,
and according to the appointed time thereof, every
year. And that these days should be remembered and
kept throughout every generation, every family, every
province, and every city. And that these days of
Purim should not fail from among the Jews, nor the
memorial of them perish from their seed.

> Book of Esther, 9:26-28

Women have to read the Book of Esther for they also
were a part of this miracle.

> Bab. Talmud Megillah, 4A

Rava says: People should drink on the Festival of
Purim until one can no longer differentiate between
Haman and Mordechai.

> Bab. Talmud Megillah, 16B

When the month of Adar begins, the joy increases.

> Bab. Talmud Taanit, 29A

All festivals will once cease but Purim will stay on.

> Midrash to Proverbs, 9:2

FAST DAYS

The 17th of the month of Tammuz remembers the siege of Jerusalem by the Babylonians in 586 B.C.E. and the conquest of the city by the Romans in 70 A.D.

The 9th of Av is the blackest day in Jewish history. It is the day the Temple of Jerusalem was destroyed. Strangely, both destructions occurred on the same day, hundreds of years apart. In the year 586 B.C.E. King Nebukadnessar of Babylonia caused the destruction of the First Temple and in the year 70 A.D. Roman commander Titus leveled the Second Temple to the ground - all but its Western Wall. The great rebellion of Bar Kochba which fought so valiantly against the Roman oppressor from its last remaining foothold in the Fortress of Betar, fell sadly and irrevocably, on the nineth day of Av into the hands of the Roman giant, (135 A.D.) and, in 1492, on that fateful day, the rich and flourishing Jewish community of Spain was driven out of its homes by King Ferdinand and Queen Isabel and the great Inquisitor Torquemada.

The fasting on the 9th of Av has the characteristics of the fast of the Day of Atonement, whereas the other fast days (all minor ones) are observed from morning to evening only. On the 9th of Av, Jeremiah's lamentations and assorted Middle Ages Laments (among them a poem to Zion by Jehuda Halevi) are read. The Sabbath preceding the 9th of Av is called Sabbath "Chazon" (vision) after the initial word in Isaiah, the beginning of which is read on this day. The Sabbath following the 9th of Av is called Sabbath "Nachamu" (comfort) using the 40th chapter of Isaiah with which it begins. It provides the Haftarah - Prophets - reading for this day.

The 3rd of Tishri is a fast day which refers to the assassination of the Jewish Governor Gedalia, installed by Babylonia to govern the conquered Israel.

The 10th of the month of Tevet commemorates the beginning of the siege of Jerusalem.

The 13th of Adar (Taanit Esther) is the day on which Queen Esther fasted in prayer and supplication prior to approaching her husband, the king, in hopes of averting Haman's plot of a total massacre.

In the event a fast day falls on the Sabbath, the Sabbath always takes precedence and, thus, moves the fast to the following Sunday. In the case of Taanit Esther falling on a Sabbath, the fast is moved to the Thursday before. The Day of Atonement is of higher importance than the Sabbath, and its full fasting ritual and observance takes place even if it falls on the Sabbath.

> Say to all the people of the land and to the priests: When you fasted and lamented in the fifth and seventh months all these seventy years, did you fast for My benefit?
>
> Zecharia, 7:5

> Thus said the Lord of Hosts: The fast of the fourth month, the fast of the fifth month, the fast of the seventh month and the fast of the tenth month shall become occasions for joy and gladness, happy festivals for the House of Judah; but you must love honesty and integrity.
>
> Zecharia, 8:19

> Rabbi Chana Bar Bisna said in the name of Rabbi Simon the Just: Why is it said: "The Fast of the Fourth month, the Fast of the Fifth month, the Fast of the Seventh month and the Fast of the Tenth month shall become occasions for joy and gladness, happy festivals for the House of Judah" (Zecharia, 8:19). Why are these days called both fast days and days of joy and gladness and cheerful seasons? - Given peace, they will be joy and cheerful, given unrest - they will be fast days.
>
> Bab. Talmud Rosh Hashanah, 18B

> When the month of Av arrives, joy decreases.
>
> Bab. Talmud Taanit, 26B

THE SERVICE IN JUDAISM

The Jewish house of worship is called Synagogue (in Reform Jewish circles, often, Temple) or in Hebrew: Bet Haknesset. Both the Greek word (Synagogue) and the Hebrew name mean: House of Assembly. Here, the Jewish community assembles on weekdays, Sabbath days and holidays for prayer and study. In its capacity as a house of prayers it is occasionally referred to as Bet Hatefillah, The House of Prayer. As a house of study, Eastern European Jewry called it "Schul" (school), which is still the Yiddish term for Synagogue. The synagogue is open for all. It is, therefore, not by chance that many Jewish houses of prayer carry the inscription: "My house shall be called a house for prayer for all peoples." (Isaiah, 56:7).

The first point of interest upon entering the Synagogue is the eastern wall which houses the Holy Ark, decorated by an elaborate and attractive special curtain called, in Hebrew, "Parochet." The ark contains the Torah scrolls, each of which encompasses the five books of Moses, handwritten on parchment. The parchment scrolls are rolled on two wooden stems. The stems are always held together with an artistically decorated band. A mantle of velvet or silk - also artistically decorated - protects the scrolls. On the wodden top of the stems are large hand-crafted exquisite crowns of silver (as are all these decorations). A silver shield hangs on the face of the scrolls' mantle, with a small silver pointer/hand (used while reading the Torah) on a silver chain completing the scroll paraphernalia. These varied ornaments are all employed so as to emphasize the importance of the Torah and its immeasurable value. Frequent illustrations of a crown as a central object of these decorations, with or without lions surrounding it, are often found embroidered on the mantle. The Torah scrolls, now as from their inception, are written without vowels and without any form of punctuation. The reading is often done with a traditional chant called "Trop." The "Ner Tamid" (the Eternal Light) hangs in front of the ark. It is lighted at the consecration of the synagogue and shall always keep burning. Often, there is a big Chanukkiah near the ark. The cantor's pulpit, the Ammud, is placed in the truly traditional synagogues, facing the ark along with his fellow congregants. In modern synagogues the Rabbi and cantor both face the congregants. The Rabbi's pulpit is visible by all, since the service is led by him.

In orthodox synagogues the ladies and the male worshippers are seated in totally segregated fashion, at separate ends of the sanctuary. The six cornered Star of David (in Hebrew: Magen David)

NER TAMID.

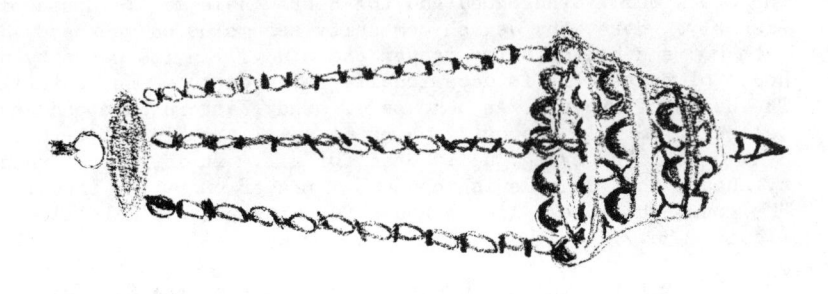

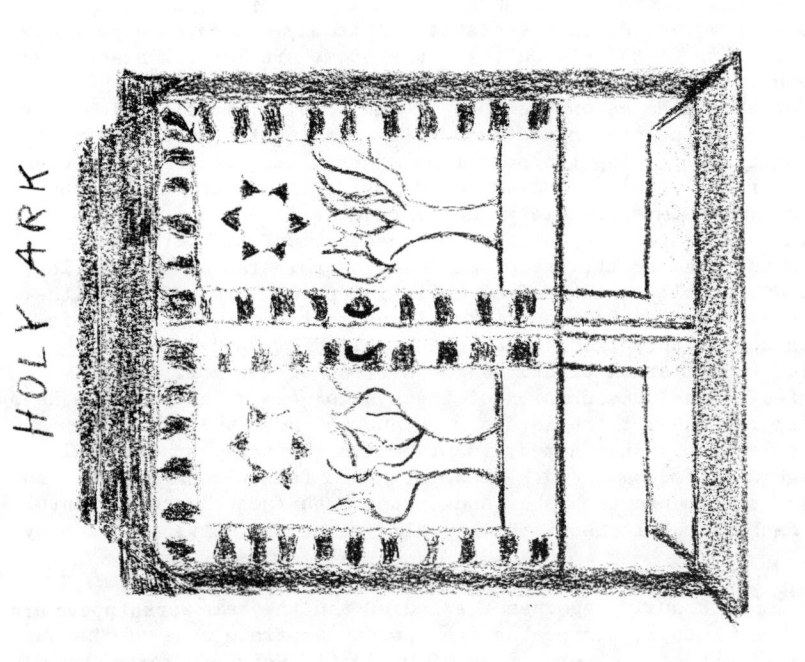

HOLY ARK

can often be found as one of the synagogue's ornaments and has, therefore, become a central symbol in Judaism. Interestingly, the Star of David is not of Jewish origin and has achieved its universal representation of Judaism in relatively recent times. A somewhat more Judaic symbol in its origin is the aforementioned "Menorah",i.e,, the seven armed candelabra. It was one of the holy objects in the holy Temple in Jerusalem, and has somehow always represented the combined Jewish concept of light and prayer. An added traditional custom, originating in the orient, in Babylonia, is the wearing of skullcaps by male worshippers, a custom practiced by all but the most reform of Reform Jews.

A community service cannot take place when there are not at least ten adult (older than 13 years) persons in attendance. (In orthodox synagogues only males; in conservative synagogues females are occasionally included in the count; in reform synagogues the females are always included). The service is based on the exchange of prayers between the cantor and the community. The cantor (Chasan in Hebrew) is considered as the representative of the prayer community (Shaliach Zibbur) and he leads the community in prayer. He may be a layman and,in theory, any Jew who knows enough Hebrew can come forward and lead. Traditionally, the service is done in Hebrew. However, in modern times congregations, especially in the conservative and reform groups,introduced an ever increasing number of prayers in the local language and for the past 150 years the organ and choir have been used in many a Synagogue as well.

The services parallel the ancient sacrifices in the Temple in Jerusalem. Hence, public prayers are said in the evening (the Maariv prayer), in the morning (Shacharit prayer), and in the afternoon (Mincha prayer). An additional prayer (Mussaf) is said after the morning prayer on Sabbath and holidays. The focal point of the morning and evening prayers is Judaism's central proclamation: "Hear, O Israel, the Lord our God, the Lord in One" - Deuteronomy, 6:4 - The "Shema" (i.e., "Hear", its first Hebrew word). In it, the Jew proclaims the unity and oneness of God. It constitutes the credo of the Judaic faith. This proclamation is followed by scriptural passages from Deuteronomy and Numbers. The first is from Deuteronomy, 4:9: "You shall love the Lord your God with all your heart, with all your soul, with all your might."

Another most important segment of the service is the Tefillah, the prayer, which is also called Amidah,because it is recited in a standing position. The afternoon and the additional prayer consist almost entirely of the Tefillah. It is a multi-faceted recitation of God's praise and contains prayers for the individual and the community. On weekdays the Tefillah (Amidah) has 19 prayers. Originally, there were 18 - therefore the name "Eighteen Prayers" (Shmone Essre). (The 19th prayer was a later addition

MAGEN DAVID.

SKULLCAP

to thwart those who turned Jews in to hostile authorities during various pogroms and persecutions). On the Sabbath and holidays, the prayers for the daily life and necessities are omitted and special Sabbath and holiday thanksgivings are included. This change gives the **Amidah** seven blessings instead of 19 on those days. The prayerbook in Judaism contains a great many Psalms, the hymns of humanity. In contrast to the Bible, the prayerbook has never been strictly fixed. It now has in it a compendium of prayers of many generations, ancient and new, including some of contemporary vintage.

The prayerbook, or Siddur, is of the greatest importance in the life of the Jewish people. No other book in Jewish literature comes so close to the life of the Jewish masses as does the Prayer Book. It was and is a daily companion, because it encompasses the whole life of earthly existence. No other volume has penetrated the Jewish home as has the Siddur.

The prayerbook for holidays which, in addition to the regular prayers, contains the special prayers for the Festivals, is called Machzor.

In Judaism, the synagogue is not only a sanctuary, but also a center for the teaching and study of Judaic subjects. Of foremost importance is the study of the proper reading of the Torah portion, which every Jew should listen to regularly. Every Sabbath and on Mondays and Thursdays a portion is read. It takes a full year to run its course and affords Jews the opportunity to go through the Books of Moses annually. On the day of the new month, on holidays and on fast days portions are read, tailored in their content, and concepts, to the occasion. On Sabbath, holidays and certain other days a chapter out of the prophets is read at the conclusion of the Torah portion. This prophets' chapter is called Haftarah (Conclusion). In its ideas and themes it contains that which was discussed in the weeks portion, whether an ordinary Sabbath or a festival.

The sermon can be both instruction or topical, covering new or old interpretations of the day's issues and current events. It is always spoken in the local language.

During every morning prayer and the Day of Atonement's evening service, the Jew wears a prayer shawl (Tallit) on the four sides of which are characteristic fringes (Tzitzit). The commandment requiring these fringes is found in the fourth book of Moses, Numbers, 15:37 in the third paragraph which follows the Shema. On weekday mornings, adult men put on phylacteries (Tefillin) on their left arm and on the forehead, in concurrence with the words in the Shema prayer: "And thou shalt bind them for a sign upon thy hand, and they shall be for frontlets between thine eyes" (Deuter-

SIDDUR.

TORAH

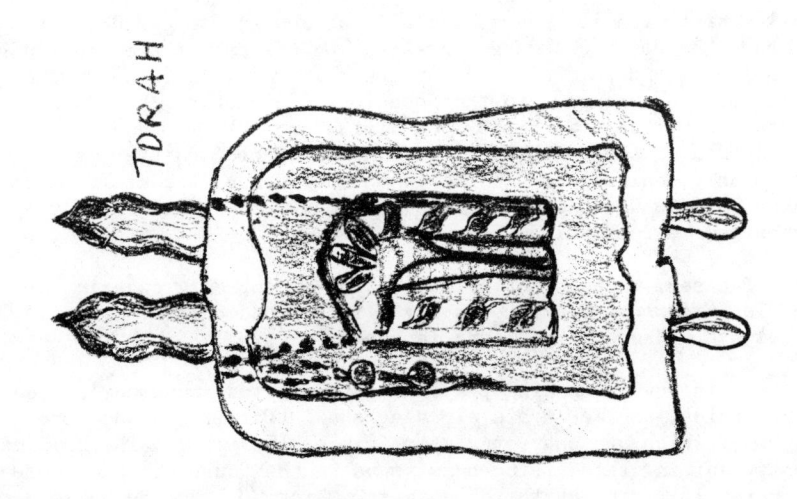

onomy, 6:8). In the two cubical boxes of leather of the phylacteries are small parchment scrolls on which the appropriate Biblical commandment has been handwritten by a scribe. The symbolic meaning of the commandment is that the head, the hand and the heart shall be devoted to God's will.

In Judaism, the prayer is not restricted to the synagogue. One can pray at any location, although it is preferable to do it as a community. Certain prayers like the Kaddish, the memorial for the dead, can only be recited in a public service (i.e., with Minjan of at least ten adults). Grace after meals and the prayers prior to retiring for the night are recited at home. Many blessings are said for various physical and spiritual experiences. Through these blessings Judaism stresses the concept that all of life and its occurences are filled with the divine presence.

> O Lord, open Thou my lips, and my mouth shall declare Thy praise.
>
> Psalms, 51:17
>
> How lovely are Thy tabernacles, O Lord of hosts; Happy are they that dwell in Thy house. They are ever praising Thee. Sela.
>
> Psalms, 85:2,5
>
> The Lord is nigh unto all them that call upon Him, to all that call upon Him in truth.
>
> Psalms, 145:18
>
> Rabbi Simon said: Be careful to read the Shema and to say the "Tefillah". When you pray, you shall not recite your prayer as a fixed mechanical task, but it should be an appeal for merry and grace before God.
>
> Sayings of the Fathers, 2:18
>
> Said Rabbi Chelbo in the name of Rabbi Huna: When one leaves the synagogue shall one not take long steps. Said Abbaje: When one goes to synagogue, one shall hasten.
>
> Bab. Talmud Berachot, 6B
>
> "But as for me, let my prayer be unto Thee, O Lord, in an acceptable time" (Psalms, 69:14). When is an acceptable time? When the Community prays.
>
> Bab. Talmud Berachot, 8A

When praying, know before whom you are standing.

> Bab. Talmud Berachot, 28B

Rabbi Eleazar said: Prayer followed sacrifices.

> Bab. Talmud Berachot, 32B

Rabbi Joshua ben Levi said: One shall always go early to the synagogue so that he can be counted to the first ten adults.

> Bab. Talmud Berachot, 47B

Resh Lakish said: Whoever has a synagogue in his town and does not go there to pray is called a lazy person.

> Bab. Talmud Berachot, 47B

One who sees one of Israel's great sages can say: Blessed be He who gives him who loves Him a part of His wisdom. When the sage is a non-Jew one recites: Blessed be He who gives His creature a part of His wisdom. One who sees a king, may recite: Blessed be He, who gives His creature a part of His honor.

> Bab. Talmud Berachot, 58A

"Love the Lord your God and serve Him with all your heart" (Deuteronomy, 11:13) What is the love of the heart? It is prayer.

> Bab. Talmud Taanit, 2A

The Holy One blessed be He, wants prayer from the righteous men.

> Bab. Talmud Jebamot, 64A

Said Rabbi Chisda; An old synagogue shall not be torn down before a new one is built.

> Bab. Talmud Baba Batra, 3B

When Rabbi Eleazar prayed he always used to give some poor man a coin.

> Bab. Talmud Baba Batra, 10A

One shall not taste and enjoy anything before one recites a blessing over it.

> Tossefta Berachot, 3

THE JEWISH LIFE

CIRCUMCISION

Eight days after a Jewish male child is born, circumcision (Brit Milah) takes place. The custom of circumcision is known and accepted by many people. This covenant served as a contract between Abraham, his descendants, his friends and God Himself. Adherance to this custom brings the newborn into the fold of this covenant, and its spirit and intent.

Before the circumcision ceremony, the infant is laid in a special chair, called "the chair of the prophet Elijah." Accordint to an ancient tradition, the prophet Elijah watches the male infant with special care and interest around the time of circumcision. The specialist, who performs the circumcision is called "Mohel" in Hebrew, and the one who holds the baby during the operation is called Sandek. When the father of the child thanks God, after the festive act, for this opportunity to introduce the baby into the covenant of Abraham, all those present recite the blessing: "As he now is being introduced into the covenant, may he also grow and blossom, for the study of Torah, for marriage and for good deeds." Immediately after the circumcision, the young boy receives his Hebrew name, which is often chosen after a deceased relative. If the eighth day falls on a Sabbath, the circumcision will take place on this day, a fact which illustrates the magnitude of the covenant. Clearly, it is important enough to take precedence over the Sabbath in spite of the days "no work" commandment. The name giving of a baby daughter usually takes place in the synagogue. The cantor or the rabbi reads a prayer for the parents and the baby and bestows the name upon the infant.

According to the ancient tradition, the first born son is consecrated to God, since God saved all Hebrew first born males in Egypt. The infant is traditionally redeemed from this consecrated state at the age of one month by donating a small symbol sum of money to a Kohen (i.e., a descendant of Aaron's priestly family) who, in turn, may turn over this donation to a charitable cause. This redemption of the first born son is called "Pidyon Haben" and is a festive celebration with invited guests and a fine meal - as is, of course, the celebration of the circumcision. The first born male infants of Priestly and Levite families are not redeemed, since their consecration to God is life long and irrevocable. Today, this concept of consecration is symbolic and ceremonial in its character. In the days of the Temple in Jerusalem, it was quite concrete due to the existence of an active priestly part of the people and the possibilities of a life totally devoted to God's services.

> This is my covenant, which ye shall keep, between Me
> and you and thy seed after thee: every male among
> you shall be circumsized. And he shall be circumsized
> in the flesh of your foreskin. And it shall be a
> token of a covenant between Me and you.
>
> Genesis, 17:10,11
>
> The first born of man shalt thou surely redeem. And
> their redemption - money - from a month old shalt
> thou redeem them - shall be, according to thy valuation.
>
> Numbers, 18:15,16
>
> The Roman Turnus Rufus asked Rabbi Akiba: Whose
> work is more perfect, your God's or mankind's?
> Rabbi Akiba answered: God's. Then Turnus Rufus
> said: If it is so and circumcision is your God's
> will, why has God not created man circumcized? Rabbi
> Akiba replied: Because our God wants to give us a
> commandment to test us with.
>
> Midrash Tanchuma Tasria, 7

BAR MITZVAH

At the age of thirteen a Jewish boy becomes Bar Mitzvah, i.e. "the son (or owner) of the commandment". He now is obliged and responsible to live according to the ethical Torah, as an adult Jew.

On the Sabbath following his thirteenth birthday he recites the blessing over the Torah for the first time and reads - if he is able to - a chapter from the weekly Torah portion and a chapter or section from the prophets. He also starts to wear a prayer shawl (Tallit) and phylacteries (Tefillin) (on weekdays) with his prayers. The Bar Mitzvah celebration which marks a new era in the life of a Jewish child - the change from childhood to manhood - is often a major social event for family and friends.

The Jewish girl is considered religiously mature at the age of twelve and is on that day called Bat Mitzvah, "The daughter (or owner) of the commandment." Although traditionally women did not count to the Minjan, Judaism did not intend to underestimate or underrate them. However, it was traditionally felt in Judaism that woman's position and tasks as wife and mother were of such monumental importance to the welfare and very existence of the family that they were exempt from a number of daily commandments so as to not render them ineffective at home. Judaism proudly and gratefully looks at its women as those to whom it owes its equilibrium.

Boys and girls at the age of fifteen or sixteen are frequently confirmed. Confirmation is a very festive occasion in which the just grown up youth pledges to be and to remain a true member of the Jewish belief.

> At the age of thirteen - to commandments.
>
> Sayings of the Fathers, 5:24

> In Jerusalem it was a beautiful custom to educate the young sons and daughters to adhere to the commandments. When the boy was mature the father took him to the priest or the elder so that he could bless and strengthen him and pray for him that the youth might grow up to study the Torah and to do good deeds.
>
> Tractate Sofrim, 18:5

TEFILLIN

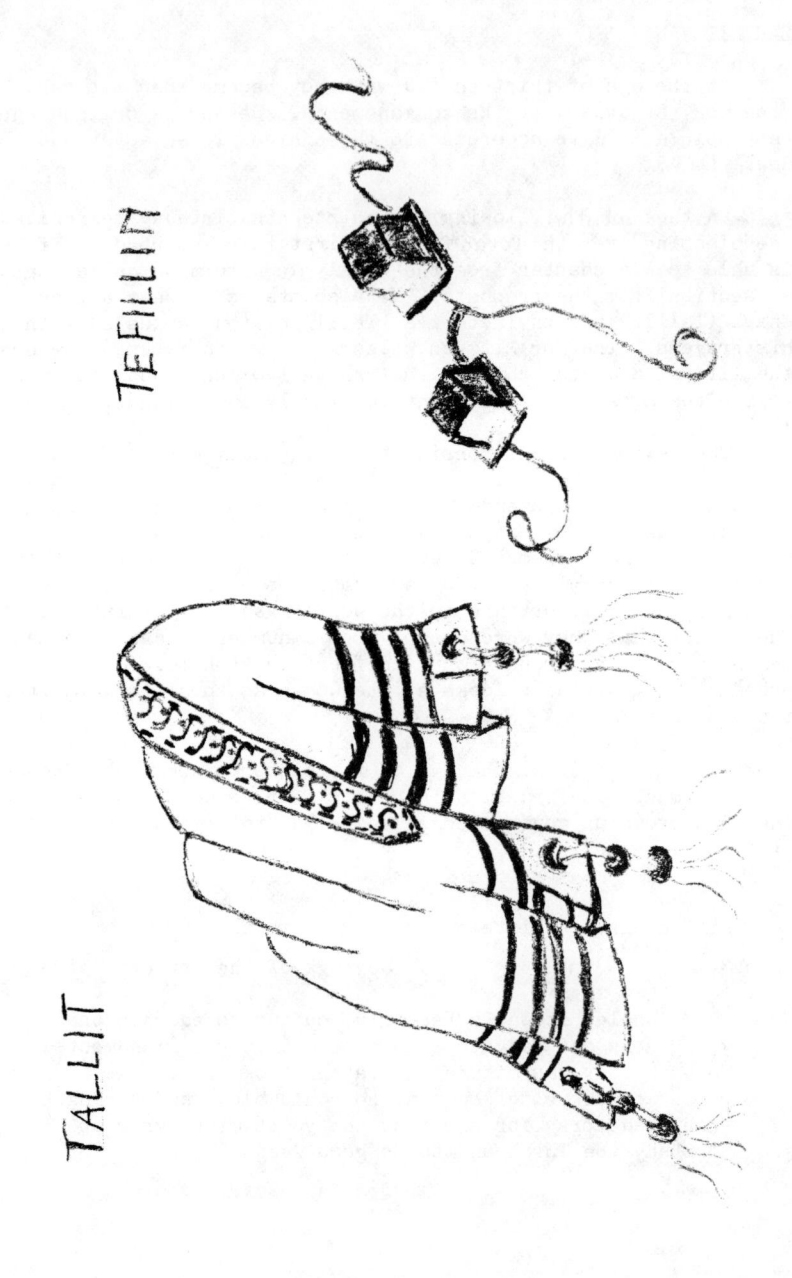

TALLIT

MARRIAGE

Since the beginning of time man and woman find each other through marriage. It is the union which permits them to do their expected share for the future of their people. Judaism would be unthinkable without this bond. The ceremony is called in Hebrew Kiddushin, "the holying", "a sacred relationship." The ceremony which is performed by a rabbi, finds the groom giving the bride a ring in the presence of two witnesses with the Hebrew words: "Be consecrated to me according to the Law of Moses and Israel", and nowadays in some circles, the bride performing the identical ceremony reciting the same verse in Hebrew. A marriage document, called Ketubah, and signed by two witnesses is read. In it the bride**groom** commits himself to care for his wife in all ways and at all times, including after death, and to be her trusted companion throughout. The ceremony takes place under a canopy (in Hebrew called Chuppah). The bride follows the groom under the canopy. The nuptial ceremony is introduced with a blessing over a goblet of wine and concludes with a blessing. There are, in all, seven blessings said:

Blessed art Thou, O Lord our God, King of the Universe, who createst the fruit of the vine.

Blessed art Thou, O Lord our God, King of the Universe, who hast created all things to Thy glory.

Blessed art Thou, O Lord our God, King of the Universe, creator of man.

Blessed art Thou, O Lord our God, King of the Universe, who hast made man in Thine image, after Thy likeness, and hast prepared unto him, out of his very self, a perpetual fabric. Blessed art Thou, O Lord, creator of man.

May she who was barren (Zion) be exceeding glad and exult, when her children are gathered within her joy. Blessed art Thou, O Lord, who makest Zion joyful through her children.

O make these loved companions greatly to rejoice, even as of old Thou didst gladden Thy creature in the Garden of Eden. Blessed art Thou, O Lord, who makest bridegroom and bride to rejoice.

Blessed art Thou, O Lord our God, King of the Universe, who hast created joy and gladness, bridegroom and bride,

CHUPPAH

mirth and exultation, pleasure and delight, love, brotherhood, peace and fellowship. Soon may there be heard in the cities of Judah, and in the streets of Jerusalem, the voice of joy and gladness, the voice of the bridegroom and the voice of the bride, the jubilant voice of bridegroom's from their canopies, and of youths from their feast of song. Blessed art Thou, O Lord, who makest the bridegroom to rejoice with the bride.

Thus, in Judaism, the community expresses its gratitude to God for the bond of marriage and prays for His blessings for the young couple. Before the nuptial ceremony, bride and groom fast in orthodox circles, however, if the marriage takes place on a day with a festive character, the fast is omitted. It is basically a symbol of the seriousness of the day for its two participants, a sort of personal Day of Atonement devoted to soul searching and turning inward.

Because marriage according to the Jewish opinion is not a sacrament it can be dissolved for some special reasons. At a divorce ceremony the man hands to his wife, in the presence of two witnesses, the letter of divorce, (in Hebrew called Gett).

And the Lord God said: It is not good that the man should be alone. I will make him a help meet for him.
Genesis, 2:18

Therefore shall a man leave his Father and his Mother, and shall cleave unto his wife, and they shall be one flesh.
Genesis, 2:24

Thy wife shall be as a fruitful vine, in the innermost parts of thy house.
Psalms, 128:3

A virtuous woman is a crown to her husband. But she that doeth shamefully is as rotteness in his bones.
Proverbs, 12:4

Whoso findeth a wife findeth a great good, and obtaineth favor of the Lord.
Proverbs, 18:22

House and riches are the inheritance of Fathers. But

a prudent wife is from the Lord.

Proverbs, 19:14

A woman of valor who can find? For her price is far above rubies.

Proverbs, 31:10

Rabbi Jacob said: One who lives without a wife, lives without happiness, without help, without joy and without blessing.

Rabbi Chiya said: Such a man is not a complete human being.

Midrash Bereshit Rabba, 17

THE JEWISH HOME

The pillars of the Jewish home are marriage and family. The Jewish dwellings have at their gate or entrance, on their upper right doorpost a decorative, small wooden or metal container in which a parchment with a Hebrew text is put. It contains the first paragraphs of the Jewish prayer "Sh**ema Yisrael**" - "**Hear**, O Israel" (Deuteronomy, 6:4-9; 11:13-20). Through a small opening in the container the word "Shaddai" shines through - "God, the Almighty." This item is called the "Mezuzah." It fulfills the commandment of keeping God's presence throughout your home and on your doorposts, emphasizing His presence in coming and going and spreading the divine countenance on the home and its members in all their endeavors.

The traditional Jewish home follows certain rules and customs concerning food consumption. With the killing of the animal intended for consumption, violence must be avoided. The slaughter is performed by a man authorized and trained in this special and compassionate skill. He is called Shochet, Slaughterer. It is strictly forbidden to consume blood and therefore the blood which remains in the meat is drawn by salt with which the meat is spread. Before its cooking the salt is washed away. Certain animals, birds and fish and all crustaceans are considered unclean and shall not be eaten. The list of permissible and non-permissible animals is found in the Pentateuch in Leviticus 11 and Deuteronomy 14. In addition, no milk and meat are to be mixed in the traditional Jewish home and consequently the keeping of separate dairy and milk dish sets and silverware are necessary. Fish is not considered as meat. The approved foods are called Kasher, i.e., "correct" or "fit" to consume. To translate it with "clean" or "hygenic" or "healthy" would be a misinterpretation of the linguistic content of the term and the intent of the commandment. Some interpreters do feel that the reasons for the laws of "Kashrut" (consumption fitness) are hygenically based, considering their times. Yet, some of the more traditional interpreters, who incidently do not totally negate the above, feel that it is the commandment to exercise a measure of restraint in order to demonstrate one's adherence to God, to His commandments and to one's own people.

Thou shalt not seethe a kid in its mother's milk.
Exodus, 23:19

This is the law of the beast, and of the fowl, and of every living creature that moveth in the waters, and of every creature that swarmeth upon the earth.

MEZUZAH

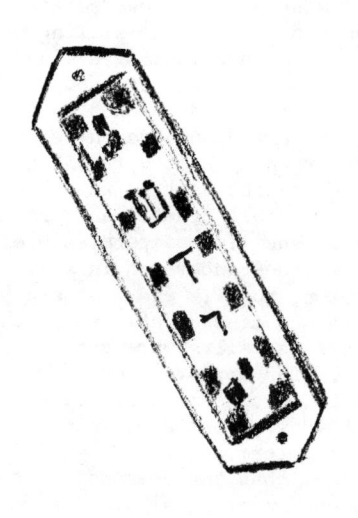

To make a difference between the unclean and the clean, and between the living thing that may be eaten and the living thing that may not be eaten.

          Leviticus, 11:46-47

Only be stedfast in not eating the blood. For the blood is the life. And thou shalt not eat the life with the flesh.

          Deuteronomy, 12:23

A prince once sent a valuable diamond as a gift to Rabbi Jehuda and let him know that he expects a present of the same value from the rabbi. Rabbi Jehuda sent him a Mezuzah. The prince sent word to the rabbi: I sent you a valuable gift and you gave me a valueless one. Rabbi Jehuda let his answer be: My present is more valuable than yours. Your gift has to be protected well so that it does not get lost. But mine protects you, your family and all who belong to your house.

          Jer. Talmud Peah, 1:1

What does it bother the Holy One, blessed be He, whether an animal is slaughtered in this or another way or whether somebody consume a clean or unclean animal. It is written: "If thou art wise, thou art wise for thyself. And if thou scornest, thou alone shalt bear it" (Proverbs, 9:12) God's commandments have been given to test man.

          Midrash Tanchuma Shemini, 12

DEATH AND MOURNING

One of the greatest commandments of Judaism is to lay to rest a deceased. Because of that there was and is in every Jewish congregation a Chevrah Kadishah, a Holy Brotherhood, whose members care for the sick and dying. A dying person shall breathe out his soul with the words "Shema Yisrael","Hear, O Israel." Those who are present at that moment recite the prayer with the dying. If a relative dies, whether near or far, the traditional blessing: "Blessed be the true justice", (God) is said. As a sign of mourning the closest relatives symbolically rent their garment (in a small way these days).

The task of the Holy Brotherhood is to wash the departed and to put him into a simple white linen garment. Men frequently get buried with their Tallit, the prayer shawl. Poor and rich are laid in the same undecorated coffin. In death no difference is exercised between persons. Some pious Jews occasionally request some soil of the Holy Land to be placed under their heads, and frequently flowers are forfeited in favor of donations to worthy causes. At the funeral, appropriate prayers are recited, and after the coffin has been lowered, those present shovel three shovels of dirt into the open grave each. When the coffin is covered with earth, the mourners say the Kaddish prayer, an Aramaic prayer in which death is not mentioned at all. Rather in it, man praises God and His many attributes and prays that His will may prevail.

The Jewish cemetery is of the greatest simplicity. The tombstones shall be free of any decoration. The eternal, undisturbed rest of the dead must be secured.

After the funeral the week of mourning begins. It is called Shivah. Children keep it for their parent, parents for their children, a husband for his wife and a wife for a husband, and brothers and sisters for their brothers and sisters. The mourners stay at home for one week, being visited by many bearing condolances and words of comfort. A worship service is conducted in the mourner's home daily. There is no mourning on the Sabbath day. On Friday evening, the beginning of the Sabbath, it is customary in many congregations to formally take in the mourners to the synagogue and to receive them with a Sabbath benediction.

The month of mourning, in Hebrew is called Shloshim (30 days) and is counted from the day of the funeral. There is no mourning during holidays. A child mourns for his or her parent one full year. During that year some maintain a candle in their home throughout the year. During eleven months mourning, offsprings say the Kaddish prayer in a public service. The annual anniversary of death is called "Jahrzeit" (the time of the year [in German]). On that day, the mourners recite the Kaddish prayer in a public service for their departed. On the first anniversary a tombstone is raised. A traditional expression used when referring to a deceased one is "Sichrono Livrachah", may his memory be blessed.

For dust thou art, and unto dust shalt thou return.
                                        Genesis, 3:19

And the dust returneth to the earth as it was, and the spirit returneth unto God who gave it.
                                        Ecclesiastes, 12:7

Rabbi Simon ben Elasar said: Do not try to comfort your fellow in a time when his deceased relative is still lying in front of him.
                                        Sayings of the Fathers, 4:23

Our sages taught: One may interrupt one's studies of the Torah to participate in a burial.
                                        Bab. Talmud Ketubot, 17A

It was said in the name of Bar Kapara: The Holy One, praised be He, counts the tears which are shed for a righteous human being and keeps them in His treasure chamber.
                                        Bab. Talmud Shabbat, 108B

TEACHINGS IN JUDAISM

Judaism is a monotheistic religion. In fact, it is **the first**, and the mother, of all monotheistic religions. It believes in one, and only one God. The Father of the Jewish people and faith, Abraham, on the order of God left his Babylonian homeland and lived as a nomad in Palestine and for a time in Egypt. He was the first who understood the concept of one God and thus, the concept of monotheism. He, who spoke to him and protected him and promised him the land where he lived as a foreigner, was not only mightier than the gods - the idols - of all the surrounding peoples, but He was for Abraham the One and Only God. So, Abraham became the first monotheist in the world where polytheism ruled with its numerous gods and goddesses. It was, in a real sense, **a** revolution in the history and thinking of mankind and of civilization. The prophets later strengthened this conception of God, enlarged and enriched it.

The one and only God in whom Judaism believes, is in His strict Oneness not a summation of the many pagan gods but in its nature something quite different. This God teaches mankind what is good and righteous and demands that a person does what is morally and ethically right. **He** shows compassion and love. The faith in Him carries also an ethical obligation. Religion and ethics belong together and cannot be divided. "Hear, O Israel, the Lord our God, the Lord is one" (Deuteronomy, 6:4) is followed by the commandment "You shall love the Lord, your God, with all your heart and with all your soul and with all your might."

Judaism is not a system of dogmas but a belief that demands that the faith be shown and fulfilled in the deed. There have been made, especially by medieval Jewish religious thinkers and philosophers, attempts to establish dogmas for the Jewish religion, but such "dogmas" as Maimonides' "Thirteen Principles of Faith" have not gained recognition as authoritative and binding. That might be in accordance with the tradition in Judaism that teaching alone and studying alone is not a cause or guarantee for redemption and bliss. Faith and belief in God, in His word and His will is, of course, a very important part of Jewish tradition and teaching, but the way to bliss goes over the good deeds and good acts, that is the way of the heart, the understanding and the fulfillment, not the theory or speculation without connection with real life.

Ye shall be holy; for I the Lord your God am holy.
                                                Leviticus, 19:2

Hear, O Israel, the statutes and the ordinances which
I speak in your ears this day, that ye may learn them,
and observe to do them.

> Deuteronomy, 5:1

And now, Israel, what does the Lord thy God require of
thee, but to fear the Lord thy God, to walk in all His
ways, and to love Him, and to serve the Lord thy God
with all thy heart and with all thy soul. To keep for
thy good the commandments of the Lord, and His statutes,
which I command thee this day?

> Deuteronomy, 10:12-13

He has told you, O man, what is good, and what the
Lord requires of you: Only to do justice and to
love goodness, and to walk modestly with your God.

> Micah, 6:8

Come, ye children, hearken unto me. I will teach you
the fear of the Lord.

Who is the man that desireth life, and loveth days,
that he may see good therein?

Keep thy tongue from evil, and thy lips from speaking
guile.

Depart from evil, and do good. Seek peace and pursue it.

> Psalms, 34:12-15

Not the learning is the main thing but the deed.

> Sayings of the Fathers, 2:17

One whose deeds come before his studies - his studies
are lasting. One whose studies come before his deeds -
his studies are not lasting.

> Sayings of the Fathers, 3:12

Do more than you learn.

> Sayings of the Fathers, 6:5

And it came to pass that a pagan came to Shammai and
said to him: I am willing to be converted if you can
teach me the whole Torah during the time I am standing
on one leg. He rejected him, with a staff which he had
in his hand. Then the pagan went to Hillel and he converted him. He said to him: That which is hateful to
you do not do unto your fellow human being. This is the
whole Torah, all the rest is interpretation. Go and

learn.

>Bab. Talmud Shabbat, 31A

Rabbi Simlai taught: The Torah has 613 commandments, namely 248 commandments "Thou shalt" symbolizing the 248 limbs of the body and 365 commandments "Thou shalt not" symbolzing the 365 days of the year.

The prophet Isaiah summarized the Torah into six commandments: "He who walks in righteousness, speaks uprightly, spurns profit from fraudulent dealings, waves away a bribe instead of grasping it, stops his ears against listening to infamy, shuts his eyes against looking at evil - such a one shall dwell in lofty security, with inaccessible cliffs for his stronghold with his food supplied and his drink assured." (Isaiah, 33:15-16).

The prophet Micah summarized the Torah into three commandments: "He has told you, O man, what is good, and what the Lord requires of you: Only to do justice and to love goodness, and to walk modestly with your God." (Micah, 6:8).

The prophet Isaiah also summarized the Torah in two commandments: "Keep ye justice and do righteousness; for my salvation is near to come, and my favour to be revealed" (Isaiah, 56:1).

And finally, the prophet Habakkuk summarized the Torah into one commandment: "The righteous man is rewarded with life for his fidelity" (Habakkuk, 2:4).

>Bab. Talmud Maccot, 23B

One who only *studies* the Torah, is like one who has no God.

>Bab. Talmud Avoda Sara, 17B

One who knows the teaching and does not perform them, for this it would have been better if he would not been born.

>Midrash Shemot Rabba, 40

GOD, THE CREATOR OF THE WORLD

The Bible is not a textbook for science or physics. The Bible does not compete with old or new theories about the creation of the universe. The purpose of the Holy Book is to teach religion, to tell us something about God. It is from this aspect that one should consider the biblical stories. It is the first lesson in the belief in God. It let us see His divine grace and might through the unique and majestic narration of the world's creation and existence. There is one God, the only God, who created the universe by His word. He is Judaism's God but at the same time, the God of the universe, all mankind's God, and the God of every human being. He is not bound to a special land or a special people. God created the world out of His free will and the world was good when it emerged from the creator's hand. God's work is without blemish or failure for He who is Himself the highest perfection, can only create perfection.

Judaism has been singularly jealous in guarding the uniqueness of God. It has therefore consistently refused to either assent or represent that uniqueness in any material form or to grant to any man the possibility of sharing in that uniqueness. Jewish monotheism is not only the negation of many gods but also the rejection of the personification of God on the one hand and of the deification of human beings on the other. Judaism is an ethical monotheism not predicated on a person. The ultimate is spirit, but not a person. He is one, but the mystery of this Oneness is unfathomable, although, of this Jews have always felt certain, it is indivisible into three - thirds, all part of the One, as Christianity teaches. Judaism has always had the philosophy of a personal God, although He was never degraded into person. It is important to realize the true meaning of a personal God who is in no respect identical with a personified God. Belief in a personal God is predicated on the conviction that the Creator of the universe, though superior to and exalted above man, is yet near and accessible to him. This belief, however, is not dependent upon the assumption that God is a person or possessed of the traits and characteristics generally associated with man. It is for this reason that Judaism has been insisting upon keeping the domain of God and the realm of man apart. This is why,from its very inception,it has denied the possibility of any man's, even the most perfect, attaining Divine perfection. To Judaism, man is man and God is God and shall remain God in unequalled and eternal majesty.

Religion and science have their places and ought to respect each other. It is senseless to try to interpret the biblical creation story scientifically and to explain the creation "days"

as millions of years or as geological periods. Science ought to
remember that there are also other answers on eternal questions
than those given by it - others in every epoch. The scientific
cosmology (view of the world) can not substitute for a religious
one. The great scientists in all centuries knew how insignificant science's absolutely secure results are. The biblical
creation stories speak not so much to the intellect and the brain
than to the heart. The narration in the Old Testament stands in
deep admiration before creation and generates the majesty of the
Creator.

In the beginning God created the heaven and the earth.

Genesis, 1:1

And God saw everything that He had made, and, behold,
it was very good.

Genesis, 1:31

Thus said God the Lord, who created the heavens and
stretched them out, who spread out the earth and
what it brings forth, who gave breath to the people
upon it, and life to those who walk thereon.

Isaiah, 42:5

He made the earth by His might, established the
world by His wisdom, and by His understanding
stretched out the skies.

Jeremiah, 10:12

By the word of the Lord were the heavens made; and
all the hosts of them by the breath of His mouth.
He gathereth the waters of the sea together as a
heap. He layeth up the deeps in storehouses. Let
all the earth fear the Lord. Let all the inhabitants
of the world stand in awe of Him. For He spoke and
it was. He commanded, and it stood.

Psalms, 33:6-9

Of old Thou didst lay the foundation of the earth;
And the heavens are the work of Thy hands.

Psalms, 102:26

And God saw everything that He had made and, behold,
it was very good. (Genesis, 1:31) To this, Rabbi
Chamma Bar Chanina gave a story. A king had
built a palace for himself, when it was finished
he went to it and said enthusiastically: O,
you my palace, may I always enjoy you as

much as I do in this moment. It is like that, that the Holy One, blessed be He, told the world: O, my world, may you always give me as much joy as on the day I created you.

Midrash Bereshit Rabba, 9

Once a man came to Rabbi Akiba and said to him: Who created the world? Rabbi Akiba answered: The Holy One, blessed be He. Said the man: You have to prove that to me. Rabbi Akiba replied: Come again tomorrow. The next day the man came back. Rabbi Akiba asked him: What do you have on you? He answered: An attire. So, Rabbi Akiba asked: Who made it? He answered: The weaver. Rabbi Akiba remarked: I do not believe you, you have to prove that to me. The man replied: How could I prove that to you, don't you know that the weaver weaves attires? Then Rabbi Akiba said to him: And you do not know that the Holy One, blessed be He, created the world? The man left. The students then said to Rabbi Akiba: And where is there the proof? Rabbi Akiba told them: My sons, like the house witnesses the builder and an attire and dresses the weaver thus the world witnesses the Holy One, blessed be He who created it.

Midrash Teruma, 26

GOD'S REVELATION

God is not only the Creator of the Universe, not only gave it His eternal law. He did not retreat from His creation. God did not abandon the world or leave it to itself, but always reveals Himself anew to mankind. He talked to the people of the Bible and revealed Himself to them in their nightly dreams. Moses saw the wondrous flame of the burning bush and heard God's voice talk to him. The revelation at Sinai during the wanderings through the desert was an experience which changed the course of the world. In a historic moment of mankind's existence the **whole people of** Israel, God's people, heard God's voice from heaven for the first time - an experience, outside the laws of nature, for which man does not have to look for a rational explanation.

The classical prophecy is a similar experience. The prophet is not a superman, not a soothsayer, not a teller of the future. He is a human being, obsessed by God and His ethical and moral commandments, who has to tell the word and ethical demands of God, even if it is against the feelings and the prevailing current among the people. He is the person chosen by God to fulfill a divine task. Moses was the greatest among the prophets to whom God spoke "from face to face." How the finite man can live up to such a contact with the infinite or how and why God chooses this one or that one for His prophet, His spokesman, His mouthpiece, is not known, not understood. There is no parallel to the classical Hebrew prophecy of the Old Testament in the history of mankind. Judaism's special standing among the people of the earth lies just therein that God has called on this people and revealed Himself to it and that among this people there were human beings who talked and acted on God's command. They were the most vigorous and most determined representatives of God's ethical and moral and social demands to mankind. Their teachings gave Judaism and the monotheistic religions their outspoken ethical sign.

(Within Christianity the first and the second commandment are counted as one, the tenth is divided into two.)

And God spoke all these words, saying:

1. I am the Lord thy God, who brought thee out of the Land of Egypt, out of the house of bondage.

2. Thou shalt have no other gods before Me. Thou shalt not make unto thee a graven image, nor any manner of likeness, or any thing that is in heaven above, or that is in the earth beneath, or that is in the water under the earth. Thou shalt not bow

down unto them, nor serve them, for I the Lord, thy God, am a jealous God, visiting the iniquity of the Fathers upon the children unto the third and fourth generation of them that hate Me. And showing mercy unto the thousandth generation of them that love Me and keep My commandments.

3. Thou shalt not take the name of the Lord, thy God, in vain. For the Lord will not hold him guiltless that taketh His name in vain.

4. Remember the Sabbath day to keep it holy. Six days shalt thou labour and do all thy work, but the seventh day is a Sabbath unto the Lord, thy God, in it thou shalt not do any manner of work, thou, nor thy son, nor thy daughter, nor thy man-servant, nor thy maid-servant, nor thy cattle, nor thy stranger that is within thy gates. For in six days the Lord made heaven and earth, the sea and all that in them is, and rested on the seventh day; wherefore the Lord blessed the Sabbath day, and hallowed it.

5. Honor thy father and thy mother that thy days may be long upon the land which the Lord, thy God, gives thee.

6. Thou shalt not murder.

7. Thou shalt not commit adultery.

8. Thou shalt not steal.

9. Thou shalt not bear false witness against thy neighbor.

10. Thou shalt not covet thy neighbor's house; Thou shalt not covet thy neighbor's wife, nor his man-servant, nor his maid-servant, nor his ox, nor his donkey, nor anything that is thy neighbor's.

                                        Exodus, 20:1-15

And He said: Hear now My words: If there is a prophet among you, I the Lord do make Myself known unto him in a vision, I do speak with him in a dream. My servant Moses is not so. He is trusted in all My house. With him do I speak mouth to mouth, even manifestly, and not in dark speeches. And the similitude of the Lord doth he behold.

                                        Numbers, 12:6-8

In the year that King **Uzziah** died, I beheld my Lord
seated on a high and lofty throne; and the skirts
of His robe filled the Temple. Seraphs stood in
attendance on Him. Each of them had six wings:
with two he covered his face, with two he covered
his legs, and with two he would fly. And one would
call to the other, "Holy, holy, holy! The Lord of
Hosts! His presence fills all the earth!" The doorposts would shake at the sound of the one who called,
and the House kept filling with smoke. I cried,
"Woe is me; I am lost! For I am a man of unclean
lips and I live among a people of unclean lips; yet my
own eyes have beheld the King Lord of Hosts." Then
one of the seraphs flew over to me with a live coal,
which he had taken from the altar with a pair of
tongs. He touched it to my lips and declared, "Now
that this has touched your lips, your guilt shall
depart and your sin be purged away." Then I heard
the voice of my Lord saying, "Whom shall I send? Who
will go for us?" And I said, "Here am I; send me?"

Isaiah, 6:1-8

The word of the Lord came to me: Before I created
you in the womb, I selected you; Before you were
born, I consecrated you; I appointed you a prophet
concerning the nations. I replied: Ah, Lord God!
I don't know how to speak, for I am still a boy. And
the Lord said to me: Do not say, "I am still a boy,"
but go wherever I send you and speak whatever I command
you. Have no fear of them, for I am with you to deliver
you - declared the Lord. The Lord put out His hand and
touched my mouth, and the Lord said to me: Herewith I
put my own words into your mouth. See, I appoint you
this day over nations and kingdoms: To uproot and
to pull down, to destroy and to overthrow, to build
and to plant.

Jeremiah, 1:4-10

"And the writing was the writing of God, graven
upon the tables." (Exodus, 32:16) Do not read
charut, graven, but cherut, Freedom. Nobody is
free except the one who accepts the teachings.

Sayings of the Father, 6:2

Not only to Israel, but to all the peoples, God
revealed Himself to give them His commandments.
First He came to Esau's descendants and said to
them: Are you willing to accept the commandments
for yourselves? What is written in them? they asked.

The Lord answered: Thou shalt not murder. They answered: Go away. Shall we cease to use the blessing which Isaac gave to our forefather Esau and which says: "And by thy sword shalt thou live." (Genesis, 27:40)

Then the Lord God went to all the other peoples and asked them: Are you willing to take My teachings upon you? And all replied: We are not interested in these commandments.

At the end He came to Israel and they answered: "All that the Lord has spoken will we do, and obey." (Exodus, 24:7)

>Midrash Pesikta Rabba, 21

Rabbi Abbahu said in the name of Rabbi Jochanan: When the Lord revealed His commandments, no fish swam, no bird flew, no ox bellowed, the angels rested in heaven, no living thing uttered a sound. The whole world was mute and still, only a mighty voice called: "I am the Lord, thy God."

> Midrash Shemot Rabba, 29

"Who would not **revere You,** O King of the nations?" (Jeremiah, 10:7) The prophets said to Jeremiah: Why do you say: King of the Nations? All the prophets call Him Israel's King and you call Him King of the Nations. He replied: I heard it from Himself: **I appointed you a prophet concerning the nations" (Jeremiah, 1:5) and** that is why I also say: King of the Nations.

> Midrash Shemot Rabba, 29

At the moment when Israel stood at the mountain of Sinai and spoke the words: "All that the Lord has spoken will we do, and obey" at that moment, there was no sick, handicapped, no limping and no blind, no mute and no deaf and no mentally disturbed.

> Midrash Vayikra Rabba, 16

All the prophets start with chastizing and ethical demands and moral wrath and finish with consolations and comfort.

> Midrash to Psalm 4

GOD AS REDEEMER AND THE MESSIANIC AGE

The world which God created and which is the place for God's revelation is not perfect as long as mankind in it is imperfect and mankind does not really understand its task to have a fellowship with the Creator of this world. Yet, the world was created to be perfect and it yearns for redemption and deliverance from failings and imperfections for the time and the age which God will bring about, whenever He wants it. The whole universe, every human soul hopes, according to the teachings of Judaism for the Mashiach, in the Greek form called (in English) Messiah, an anointed one, of King David's family, who shall come to rule the world, to deliver it and every human being. The Messiah will bring about for the universe eternal love, eternal brotherhood, justice and friendship. There will be no bloodshed anymore, no wars, not even in nature among the beasts and eternal peace will prevail in the world. All mankind shall then recognize Israel's God as the only Lord and serve Him in faithfulness and righteousness. The people will live on in the messianic age, they will make an eternal covenant and violence and injustice will for all times be banned. All the people will then turn with grateful and willing hearts to Zion, the mountain of the Lord, "For instruction shall come forth from Zion, the word of the Lord from Jerusalem" (Isaiah, 2:3).

How far the world is today from God and how long away from His redemption, can be seen clearest in Israel's lot. A great part of the Jewish people live in the diaspora and suffer very often from persecution and even genocide. When the Messiah comes to deliver the world, he shall, according to the tradition, collect the various dispersed members of the people of Israel from all the lands of the earth and bring them to the Land of Israel. There are various thoughts within the Rabbinic literature about the resurrection of the dead after the times of the Messiah's arrival. Some say there will be a resurrection but others insist that not the age of the Messiah but the so-called "coming world" is the contrast to this world, man's life on earth.

The prophets were the first who visioned such a time and age. First and foremost it was the great and mighty Isaiah who introduced this inspiring idea to mankind. It was a thought which proved to be a stimulance for progress in all times. Later both the rationalistic and mystic thoughts were knotted to the ancient Jewish Messiah's hopes. There is talk about a grim and devestating war period which shall precede the messianic age and that there might be one who first will appear to announce the coming of the Messiah. This might be the prophet Eliah who will return to earth before the Messiah comes. In any case, in Judaism the Messiah is not and will not be God. He is sent by God, a messenger of God. In times of sufferings - in many parts of the diaspora - the yearning for deliverance and the hope for redemption, for the Messiah, arose and was sometimes elevated to desperate certainty: Now he shall come, now he must be it. False Messiah figures appeared often, therefore, in the history of Judaism and gave to the persecuted and suffering the straw and the great hope they were looking for, but then they were let down in doubt and deep desperation. Many prayers in Judaism give expression to the messianic thought. That does not mean a backup to the beginning of the world, but a deep hope towards the purpose of creation.

> In the days to come, the Mount of the Lord's House shall stand firm above the mountains and tower above the hills; and all the nations shall gaze on it with joy. And the many peoples shall go and shall say: "Come, let us go up to the Mount of the Lord, to the House of the God of Jacob; that He may instruct us in His ways, and that we may walk in His paths." For instruction shall come forth from Zion, the word of the Lord from Jerusalem. Thus He will judge among the nations and arbitrate for the many peoples and they shall beat their swords into plowshares and their spears into pruning hooks: Nation shall not take up sword against nation; they shall never again know war.
>
> Isaiah, 2:2-4

> But a shoot shall grow out of the stump of Jesse, a twig shall sprout from his stock. The spirit of the Lord shall alight upon him: A spirit of wisdom and insight, a spirit of course and valor, a spirit of devotion and reverance for the Lord. He shall sense the truth by his reverence for the Lord: He shall not judge by what his eyes behold nor decide by what his ears perceive. Thus he shall judge the poor with equity and decide with justice for the lowly of the land. He shall strike down a land with the rod of his mouth and slay the wicked with the breath of his lips. Justice shall be the girdle of his loins, and faithfulness the girdle of his waist. The wolf shall dwell with the lamb, the leopard lie down with the kid; the calf, the beast of prey, and the fatling together, with a little boy to herd them. The cow and the bear shall graze, their young shall lie down together; and the lion, like the ox, shall eat straw. A babe shall play over a viper's hole, and an infant pass his hand over an adder's den. In all of My sacred mountain nothing evil or vile shall be done; for the land shall be filled with

devotion to the Lord as water covers the sea.

>   Isaiah, 11:1-10

I am bringing My victory close; it shall not be
far, and My triumph shall not be delayed. I will
grant triumph in Zion to Israel in whom I glory.

>   Isaiah, 46:13

O Lord, my strength and my stronghold, my refuge in
a day of trouble, to you nations shall come from the
end of the earth and say: Our Fathers inherited
utter delusions, things that are futile and worthless.

>   Jeremiah, 16:19

And the Lord shall be King over all the earth. In that
day there shall be one Lord with one name.

>   Zechariah, 14:9

When Rabbi Akiba saw Bar Kochba he said: This is
the King, the Messiah. But Rabbi Jochanan said to
him: Akiba, grass will grow in your hands before
the descendant of David will reveal himself.

>   Jer. Talmud Taanit, 4:7

Rabbi Joshua ben Levi one day found the prophet
Eliah standing at the entrance of his cave. He asked
the prophet: When will the Messiah come? Eliah answered:
You may ask him himself. - Whereupon Rabbi
Joshua: Where is he? - At the gate of Rome. - And how
does one recognize him? - He sits among the sick and
cares for their wounds - Rabbi Joshua traveled to the
Messiah and greeted him with the words: Peace be with
you, my Lord and Master. The Messiah replied: Peace be
with you, Levi's son. Rabbi Joshua asked: When, O
Lord, will you reveal yourself? - He answered: Today.

Rabbi Joshua went back to the prophet Eliah, who asked
him: What did he say? - He told me a lie because he
said that he will come today and he did not come. Then
the prophet said: With that he wanted to tell you:
"Today, if you will listen to his voice."

>   Bab. Talmud Sanhedrin, 98A

Rabbi Hillel said: Israel cannot expect another
Messiah after Israel already experienced the messianic
age during King Hiskiah's days. Rabbi Joseph then said:
God forgive Rabbi Hillel! When did King Hiskiah live?
That was at the time of the first Temple. And the prophet

Zecharia who prophesied in the time of the second Temple, spoke out as follows: "Rejoice greatly, fair Zion, raise a shout, fair Jerusalem! Lo, your king is coming to you." (Zechariah, 9:9).

> Bab. Talmud Sanhedrin, 99A

When you see the empires go up to fight against each other, then you may hope that the Messiah is near.

> Midrash Bereshit Rabba, 42

If Israel does not atone it will not be redeemed. Yet, Israel will not be brought to atonement but by sufferings, oppression and persecution.

> Pirke Rabbi Eliezer, 43

Whoever tries to ascertain the end of time, has lost his right for his place in the eternal life.

> Derech Eretz Sutta, 11

And to Jerusalem, Thy city, return in mercy, and dwell therin as Thou hast spoken. Rebuild it soon in our days as an everlasting building and speedily set up therein the throne of David. Blessed art Thou, O Lord, who rebuildest Jerusalem. Speedily cause the offspring of David, Thy servant, to flourish, and lift up his glory by Thy divine help because we wait for Thy salvation all the day. Blessed art Thou, O Lord, who causest the strength of salvation to flourish.

> Daily Prayer:
> The Eighteen Benedictions

May the All-merciful make us worthy of the days of the Messiah, and of the life of the world to come.

> Grace After Meals

Gladden us, O Lord our God, with Eliah the prophet, Thy servant, and with the kingdom of the House of David, Thine anointed. Soon may he come and rejoice our hearts. Suffer not a stranger to sit upon his throne, not let others any longer inherit his glory. For by Thy holy name Thou didst swear unto him that his light should not be quenched for ever. Blessed art Thou, O Lord, the shield of David.

> Sabbath Morning Service:
> The Haftarah Blessing

Magnified and sanctified by His great name in the world which He has created according to His will. May He establish His kingdom during your life and during your days, and during the life of all the house of Israel, even speedily and at a near time, and say ye: Amen.

       Kaddish Prayer

Give then glory, O Lord, unto Thy people, praise to them that revere Thee, hope to them that seek Thee, and confidence to them that wait for Thee, joy to Thy land, gladness to Thy city, a flowering of strength unto David Thy servant, and a clear shining light unto the son of Jesse, Thine anointed, speedily in our days.

       Prayer for the New Year's Day
       and the Day of Atonement

GOD AND MAN

After God revealed Himself to Moses at Mount Sinai, Moses asked to be allowed to see God's presence. But God said to him: "Thou canst not see My face, for man shall not see Me and live.... And thou shalt see My back. But My face shall not be seen" (Exodus, 33:20,23). Does God have a face? How can one speak of God's back, eyes or ears: It is in fact man, who describes God in a human figure, a human way and with human virtues. Such "anthropomorphism" is possible and even unavoidable, because the human language is unable to really express God's nature. There is a personal God in Judaism, a God who is near and reachable by a person. Yet, there is absolutely no personified God in the concept of Judaism, a God who has the elements of a person, a human being in his nature. That is the essence in God's reply to Moses: No human being of flesh and blood, not even Moses, the greatest and closest to God among the prophets, can see "My Face", that means, really get God's nature. Man can only see God's "back", meaning, man can only see and understand God through His work.

For in order to see God and really understand His working, it would be necessary for man to be himself divine. One can only really understand his own likeness. An animal can hardly, really, understand the nature and working and thinking of man. It can only understand what it sees from his deeds. In the same sense, man must also content himself with the idea that he cannot completely understand what God is. He calls Him the Holy One, the Almighty, who through His work teaches man to understand the demands and commandments He asks from him. It is man's task to make holy his own life, to fulfill the ethical and moral commandments of God as much as he can, because God is holy. It is man's task to strive for perfection as much as possible, because God is perfect. It is for that purpose that God reveals Himself to man through His work. The soul of man is, according to Judaism, immortal and insofar blessed with a divine nature, which means that it has the ability to understand the demands of God which can lead it to higher perfection.

God is not only the creator of the universe and its king, but also the Father of each individual, the shield and protector of each one. He is the Lord of the world and of the individual being in it. He is the God of righteousness and in a hither sense the God of Love. Man can always renew the living companionship with his God. In Judaism, man has a direct relationship with God. It is a real "I and Thou" relationship. There is no savior or redeemer or priest or intermediary between the individual Jew and his God. He shows mercy for good deeds unto many generations. The righteousness of the Forefathers is remembered to coming generations "unto the thousandth generation of them that love Me and keep My commandments."

Man can always hope for Him and His support. He was and has been and is man's light to life and progress.

> Commit thy way unto the Lord. Trust also in Him, and He will bring it to pass.
>
> Psalms, 37:5

> Lord, Thou hast been our dwelling-place in all generations. Before the mountains were brought forth, or ever Thou hast formed the earth and the world, even from the everlasing to everlasting, Thou art God. Thou turnest man to contrition, and sayest: Return, ye children of men.
>
> Psalms, 90:1-3

> Like a father has compassion upon his children, so has the Lord compassion upon them that fear Him.
>
> Psalms, 103:13

> O Lord, Thou hast searched me, and known me. Thou knowest my downsitting and mine uprising. Thou understandest my thought a far off. Thou measurest my going about and my lying down, and art acquainted with all my ways. For there is not a word in my tongue, but Lo, O Lord, Thou knowest it altogether. Thou hast hemmed me in behind and before and laid Thy hand upon me. Such knowledge is too wonderful for me, too high, I cannot attain unto it. Whither shall I go from Thy spirit? Or whither shall I flee from Thy presence? If I ascend up into heaven, Thou are there, if I make my bed in the netherworld, behold, Thou art there.
>
> Psalms, 139:1-8

> Rabbi Elazar said: Until the last minute of his death the Holy One, blessed be He, has mercy with man and waits for his remorse.
>
> Bab. Talmud Pessachim, 87B

The Emperor said to Rabbi Joshua ben Chananja: I want to see your God. He replied to the Emperor: You cannot see Him. The Emperor answered: Nevertheless, I want to see Him. Then Rabbi Joshua turned the Emperor towards the sun. The Emperor said: I cannot stand that. -

Rabbi Joshua then told him: The sun is only a creation and a messenger of the Holy One, blessed be He, and you say you cannot stand it to look at it, how much less could you see the Lord, the Almighty.

> Bab. Talmud Chulin, 60A

Man mints many mints, the same tool, and all of them are alike. The King of Kings, the Holy One, blessed be He, creates every human being and yet not one is exactly like the other.

> Bab. Talmud Sanhedrin, 37A

Wherever the divine name "Lord" appears, it means mercy: "The Lord, the Lord, merciful and gracious, long-suffering, and abundant in goodness and truth" (Exodus, 34:6).

> Midrash Bereshit Rabba, 33

How many wonderworks does the Holy One, blessed be He, for man and he knows nothing about it.

> Midrash Shemot Rabba, 24

GOD AND EVIL

Judaism is a religion of optimism. It believes in the good, in the one, good God who created the good for mankind's sake. Yet, does the Bible and Judaism not also know of the evil force? Is there not, for instance, in the book of Job a figure with the name of Satan? Satan, the accuser, belongs in the book of Job to the vicinity of God as a subordinate. He stands, like the other angels, under the laws and rules of God. And when he wants to test Job's fear of God, he can do this only with God's permission. Satan is not an independent principle against God, but representant of the evil from His hand. Both the good and the evil are put before the individual and he or she is given the opportunity and the ability to weigh, judge and choose freely between the two.

When evil is no longer only a turning away from the good, but is itself considered as the good, then the moral universe and the ethical concept of the civilized world have been turned upside down and the sovereignty of evil has been established. To call evil good, to consider murder and brutal, senseless killing meritorious is to proclaim that God and the good in His creation has been substituted by the evil, by Satan.

This was the logic of the Holocaust. This celebration of death by the Nazis which cost eleven million men, women and children their lives - among them six million Jews - spread the rule of evil over a generation and turned the epoch into an age of darkness.

The Holocaust, also known in Hebrew as the Shoah, the Catastrophe, is the most tragic period of Jewish history and, maybe, of modern mankind. The nature and the systematic and thorough planning and execution of this crime of genocide is unique. The consequences of the Holocaust - which cannot and must never be forgotten - are of decisive significance for the Jewish present and future: those consequences are evident today and will be experienced for generations to come.

The presence of evil, to be avoided by man, is necessarily the reason for the existence of ethics. Would the way of life only be good, it would be of no special merit to strive for it. Jewish ethics are predicted on the trust in man's ethical freedom, the faculty of choice between good and evil. Man is not dragged down by "original sin" and therefore no special act of "grace" is necessary. Free decision is the very foundation of the ethics of Judaism, for without the temptation and the possibility to sin, piety would not be meritorious. Only through the free will to choose between that which God loves and that which He hates can man develop and evolve, according to Jewish teachings, into an ethical and moral creature.

As stated previously, Judaism does not consider man as born with "original sin." Additionally, the Bible says that "the imagination of man's heart is evil from his youth" (Genesis, 8:20). i.e., the child at birth knows only good, but during his youth, the young one sees and learns evil and, then, learns and understands to differentiate between good and evil. To be able to do that, means that new perspectives are opened for the young human being. Through the "good inclination" the human being is elevated over the animal which only knows the primitive inclination. The human being should understand neither the good nor the evil inclination as a force which excludes the human freedom. Freedom is given and the one who uses it properly, in the right way, will never miss the reward.

The individual who has been victorious over evil and whose ways are righteous is honored with a name which the Bible even gave God: Such an individual is a "righteous one."

See, I have set before thee this day life and good, and death and evil, in that I command thee this day to love the Lord, thy God, to walk in His ways, and to keep His commandments and His statutes and His ordinances.
> Deuteronomy, 30:15-16

The path is level for the righteous man. O Just One, You make smooth the course of the righteous.
> Isaiah, 26:7

I form light and create darkness, I make weal and create woe - I the Lord do all these things.
> Isaiah, 45:7

For the work of a man will He requite unto him, and cause every man to find according to his ways. Yea, of a surety, God will not do wickedly, neither will the Almighty pervert justice.
> Job, 34:11-12

Light is sown for the righteous, and gladness for the upright in heart.
> Psalms, 97:11

The righteous is an everlasting foundation.

> Proverbs, 10:25

Who is mighty? He who subdues his passions.

> Sayings of the Fathers, 4:1

Rabbi Jochanan said: Hail Israel! As long as they study, are busy with and do the commandments of the teachings and the law and do good deeds, they rule the sin and the sin does not rule them.

> Bab. Talmud Avoda Sara, 5B

"Happy is the man" (Psalms, 1:1) - Happy is the human being who is victorious over his evil inclination.

> Bab. Talmud Avoda Sara, 19A

The thought of sin is more dangerous than the sin itself.

> Bab. Talmud Yoma, 29A

Said Rabbi Elazar: The universe could have been created even for the righteous one's sake - Said Rabbi Chija Bar Abba in the name of Rabbi Jochanan: Yes, for one righteous one's sake is the universe kept because it is written: "The righteous is an everlasting foundation" (Proverbs, 10:25).

> Bab. Talmud Yoma, 38B

Said Rabbi Jochanan: The righteous are greater than angels.

> Bab. Talmud Sanhedrin, 92A

Said Rabbi Bar Chana: The soul of only one righteous equals the whole world.

> Bab. Talmud Sanhedrin, 103B

Said Rabbi Chamma Bar Chanina: The righteous is bigger in his death than in his life.

> Bab. Talmud Chullin, 7B

One does not set tombstones for the righteous. Their words and deeds are eternal signs of remembrance.

> Jer. Talmud Shekalim, 2:5

Said Rabbi Samuel Bar Nachman: "And God saw everything that He had made, and, behold, it was good" (Genesis, 1:31) - that is the good inclination. "It was very good" - that is the evil inclination. How can the evil inclination be good? - This will teach you: if the evil inclination would not be there, man would not build houses, would not marry a woman, would not have children and would not care for his sustenance.

Midrash Bereshit Rabba, 9

"For the imagination of man's heart is evil from his youth" (Genesis, 8:21). If you now say, why did the Holy One, blessed be He, create the evil inclination and if you asked for what was that good, the Holy One, blessed be He, says: It is you yourself who does the evil. Why? You were an innocent child and did not sin, now, when you grew to be an adult, you sin.

Midrash Tanchuma Bereshit

REMORSE AND ATONEMENT

Sin is, according to Judaism, not a necessary human lot, which, from the first human being in the Garden of Eden, is inherited from generation to generation. Sin does not rule man but man rules sin. Man can sin but does not have to do it. He has the force and the choice over the "evil inclination". It is man himself who creates his sin. He is also, therefore, responsible for it and he can, if he only wants to, return to his God. The human being has the free will, the choice between good and evil. And if he chooses evil, no grace can atone for it. There is an expression in Hebrew which means both remorse and atonement: Teshuva. Remorse means that man can find the way back to God in the same way as a child finds the way back to a loving father or mother. God's everlasting love stretches His hand to us every day until the last day of the life, if we only call the Lord and confess our sins before Him.

Remorse is a kind of being born again. God makes a new covenant with the new human being. God does not want the sinner's punishment or death but his remorse, his return to a better life. The sinner has only to confess and confront his transgression with honesty and real regret, to go into serious soul searching and to want with all his heart and all his soul and all his might to change, to make good, then he turns again towards God's side. That is called atonement. Before God the individual atones with himself. That God is a God of atonement, is the unique and clear consequence of His divinity. To get atonement, there is no grace or sacrifice, like in the time of the Temple in Jerusalem, necessary. The humble heart and mind substitutes for every sacrifice.

There is a connection between the thought of atonement and the messianic idea in Judaism. When mankind turns towards the One, the only God, then there will be atonement for all humanity and the messianic age is near. The idea of atonement is one of Judaism's central ideas. Judaism's holiest and greatest holiday, the Yom Kippur, the Day of Atonement, is devoted to this thought. The individual and the community consider this day as the high point of the year. It gives us God's answer to our remorse and turning and soul searching - atonement.

And all the congregation of the children of Israel shall be forgiven, and the stranger that sojourneth among them. For in respect of all the people it was done in error.
                                        Numbers, 15:26

Moreover, if the wicked man repents of all the sins
that he committed and keeps all My laws and does what
is just and right, he shall live; he shall not die.
None of the transgressions he committed shall be
remembered against him; because of the righteousness he
has practiced, he shall live. Is it My desire that a
wicked man shall die? - says the Lord God. It is rather
that he shall turn back from his ways and live. Cast
away all the transgressions by which you have offended,
and get yourselves a new heart and a new spirit, that
you may not die, O House of Israel. For it is not My
desire that anyone shall die - declares the Lord God.
Repent, therefore, and live!

> Ezekiel, 18:21-23;31-32

Good and upright is the Lord. Therefore does He
instruct sinners in the way.

> Psalms, 25:8

The sacrifices of God are a broken spirit. A broken
and a contrite heart, O God, Thou wilt not despise.

> Psalms, 51:19

For with Thee there is forgiveness, that Thou mayest
be feared.

> Psalms, 130:4

Rabbi Abahu Bar Seira said: Great is remorse for it
came before the creation of the world, as it is written:
"Before the mountains were brought forth, or ever Thou
hadst formed the earth and the world. Even from everlasting to everlasting, Thou art God. Thou turnest man
to contrition, and sayest: Return, ye children of man"
(Psalms, 90:2-3).

> Midrash to Psalm, 90

One asked wisdom: What is the punishment of the sinner?
Wisdom answered: "Evil pursueth sinners" (Proverbs,
13:21). One asked the prophet: What is the punishment of the sinner? The prophet replied: **"The person
who sins, only he shall die"**(Ezekiel, 18:4). One asked
the Torah: What is the punishment of the sinner? The
Torah said: He can bring a sacrifice and be remorseful.
One asked the Holy One, praised be He: What is the
punishment of the sinner? The Holy One, praised be He ,
said: He can turn and make atonement. As it is written:
"Good and upright is **the Lord. Therefore does He**
instruct sinners in the way" (Psalms, 25:8). He shows

the sinner the way to return.

Jalkut Shimoni to Psalm 25

Rabbi Elieser said: Turn away from sin one day before your death. His students asked him: But can a human being know when he is going to die? He answered them: Therefore he shall turn every day because perhaps he is going to die tomorrow.

Bab. Talmud Shabbat, 153A

One who says: I will sin and return, I will sin and return, for him returning will not succeed.

Bab. Talmud Yoma, 85B

Rabbi Levi said: Great is returning because it brings nearer to God's throne, as it is written: "Return, O Israel, to the Lord, thy God". (Hosea, 14:2). Rabbi Chamma the son of Rabbi Chanina said: Great is returning for it brings healing to the world, as it is written: "I will heal their affliction, generously will I take them back in love; for My anger has turned away from them" (Hosea, 14:5). Rabbi Jochanan said: Great is returning for it brings redemption with it, as it is written: "He shall come as redeemer to Zion, to those in Jacob who turn back from sin - declares the Lord" (Isaiah, 59:20).

Bab. Talmud Yoma, 86A

Said Rabbi Abahu: On the place where those who return stand, could completely righteous ones not stand, as it is written: "It shall be well, well with the far and the near". (Isaiah, 57:19). The far first, then the near.

Bab. Talmud Berachot, 34B

The Holy One, praised be He, abandons nobody who wants to atone. In every moment the door is open and one who wants, may come in.

Midrash Shemot Rabba 19

MAN AND HIS FELLOW MAN

The relationship between God and man precipitates a relationship between human beings themselves. Only in his dealings with his fellow men can man learn the right relationship with his God. One's fellow man is God's child. Hence, all men, including oneself, are brothers and sisters, offsprings of one Father and therefore equal.

Judaism has always stressed man to man relationships and man's efforts to concentrate on his fellow man more so even than the love of God himself. Man,who is only part of the totality of humanity, rather than an individual free to exploit others to his sole advantage, must jealously guard the rights of all others to be fair and equal. He also must bear the responsibilities of equality and freedom in this society.

This task is the basis for the many demands Judaism puts on the relationship between the individuals: Righteousness, love, tolerance and work for peace and understanding - ethical demands which not only refer to Jews among themselves but to universal relationships as well. Even love for animals is a commandment in Judaism. Human love is especially needed in relationship with the socially less fortunate: widows, orphans, strangers, the sick and the poor.

Mutual respect, love and compassion, can, in turn, lead to other worthy attitudes such as humility and gratitude which, in turn, can expand that which is divine in each of us. Ethical relationship towards our fellow man is the moral life God asks from us. One who pursues it, goes "God's path", as the Bible says.

> Ye shall not steal. Neither shall ye deal falsely, nor lie one to another. And ye shall not swear by My name falsely, so that thou profane the name of thy God: I am the Lord. Thou shalt not oppress thy neighbour, nor rob him. The wages of a hired servant shall not abide with thee all night until the morning.
>
> Leviticus, 19:11-13

> Thou shalt not hate thy brother in thy heart. Thou shalt surely rebuke thy neighbour and not bear sin because of him.
>
> Leviticus, 19:17

Thou shalt not take vengeance, nor bear any grudge
against the children of thy people, but thou shalt
love thy neighbour as thyself: I am the Lord.

>Leviticus, 19:18

Thou shalt rise up before the hoary head and honor the
face of the old man. And if a stranger sojourn with thee
in your land, ye shall not do him wrong. The stranger
that sojourneth with you shall be unto you as the homeborn among you and thou shalt love him as thyself. For
ye were strangers in the land of Egypt. I am the Lord
your God.

>Leviticus, 19:32-34

And if you sell aught unto thy neighbour, or buy of thy
neighbour's hand, ye shall not wrong one another.

>Leviticus, 25:14

Thou shalt not oppress a hired servant that is poor and
needy, whether he be of thy breathren or of thy strangers
that are in thy land within thy gates. In the same day
thou shalt give him his hire, neither shall the sun go
down upon it. For he is poor and setteth his heart
upon it. Lest he cry against thee unto the Lord and it
be sin in thee.

>Deuteronomy, 24:14-15

Thou shalt not have in thy bag diverse weights, a great
and a small. Thou shalt not have in thy house diverse
measures, a great and a small. A perfect and just weight
shalt thou have. A perfect and just measure shalt thou
have. That thy days may be long upon the land which the
Lord thy God giveth thee.

>Deuteronomy, 25:13-15

He has told you, O man, what is good, and what the
Lord requires of you: Only to do justice, and to love
goodness, and to walk modestly with your God.

>Micah, 6:8

Thus said the Lord of Hosts: Execute true justice;
deal loyally and compassionately with one another.
Do not defraud the widow, the orphan, the stranger,
and the poor; and do not plot evil against one another.

>Zechariah, 7:9-10

Withhold not good from him to whom it is due, when it is in the power of thy hand to do it. Say not unto thy neighbour: Go and come again and tomorrow I will give, when thou hast it by thee.

        Proverbs, 3:27-28

A false witness shall not be unpunished. And he that breatheth forth lies shall not escape.

        Proverbs, 19:5

Rejoice not when thine enemy falleth, and let not thy heart be glad when he stumbleth. Say not: I will do so to him as he has done to me. I will render to the man according to his work.

        Proverbs, 24:17, 29

When Rabbi Eliezer had finished his daily prayer, he used to add: May Thou, O Lord, our God, let love, brotherhood and peace rest in our midst.

        Bab. Talmud Berachot, 16B

Rabbi Jochanan Ben Sakkai used always first to greet one he met even the pagan at the gate.

        Bab. Talmud Berachot, 17A

One has to take care of the poor of the pagans in the same way as one takes care of the poor of the Hebrews for the sake of peace. One has to take care of the sick of the pagans in the same way as one takes care of the Hebrew sick. One has to bury the dead of the pagans in the same way as one does with the dead Hebrews.

        Bab. Talmud Gittin, 61A

"Thou shalt love thy neighbour as thyself" (Leviticus, 19:18). Said Rabbi Akiba: This is an important principle in the Torah. Said Rabbi Asai: There is a principle in the Torah which is even more important: "This is the book of the generations of Adam. In the day that God created man, in the likeness of God made He him." (Genesis, 5:1).

        Sifra to Leviticus, 19:18

"Thou shalt not take vengeance, nor bear any grudge" (Leviticus, 19:18). What does it mean to take vengeance and what to bear any grudge? If somebody wants to borrow something from you, you shall not say to him: I will not lend it to you because you would not lend to me,

that would be vengeance. Yet, neither should you
say: I will lend you what you want because I am
not like you who would not lend it to me. That
would mean to bear a grudge.

      Sifra to Leviticus, 19:18

When somebody says to you a bad word, do not answer
him. When you said a bad word to someone may it be the
humblest or the highest, apologize before you go away.
Love your fellow men and honor them.

      Derech Eretz Suta, 1

The Holy One, praised be He, said to Israel: What
is it that I demand from you? Nothing else than that
you love and honor each other.

      Tanna Debe Elijahu, 26

The human being must always strive to do good to the
living as well as to the dead.

      Midrash Leolam, 7

MAN AND HIS HOME

    The individual fulfills his life within the framework of the society. The most intimate part of the society is the family. According to Judaism, the family is the most important and essential basis of the world order because it is not only the natural perpetuation of the human race but also the chain of communication between the generations. Within the family circle the child takes over the traditions of the father in order to give them later as a heritage to his children. Judaism originated the expression "S-Chut Avot" - the privilege of the forefathers, which is a privilege that a child and coming generations receive for the fulfilling of the good deeds of their forefathers. Family life and the home of the parents and grandparents have their influence upon the whole way of life of the next generation. It is for this reason that Judaism commands that the family should be held holy and intact. It is important in Judaism that the child love and revere his parents. They are, in his formative years, his interpreters to God's words. Stiff penalties are suggested by the Torah for those who disobey this important commandment. It is, on the other hand, the parents' most important duty to give the child the best education possible.

    The family unit is the basis for the next family unit. In Judaism the bond of marriage of a family is the love and trust and comradship between man and woman. It is only man AND wife who deserve the honor to be called "man". The marriage ceremony is called with the Hebrew word of "Holiness" (or "The Holying") and the wife is often within the rabbinical Judaism called "my house". Mankind shall be tested in marital faithfulness and marital responsibilities for coming generations. Man and wife are equal within Judaism, in terms of their parental duties and responsibilities. Although in ancient times equality might not always have been present, it is the way of life today.

    And the Lord said: It is not good that the man should be alone, I will make him a help meet for him.
                                             Genesis, 2:18

    Therefore shall a man leave his father and his mother, and shall cleave unto his wife and they shall be one flesh.
                                             Genesis, 2:24

Ye shall fear every man his mother and his father.

> Leviticus, 19:3

Cursed be he that dishonoreth his father or his mother. And all the people shall say: Amen.

> Deuteronomy, 27:16

A wise son maketh a glad father. But a foolish man despiseth his mother.

> Proverbs, 15:20

Whoso findeth a wife findeth a great good, and obtaineth favor of the Lord.

> Proverbs, 18:22

House and riches are the inheritance of fathers. But a prudent wife is from the Lord.

> Proverbs, 19:14

Whoso curseth his father or his mother, his lamp shall be put out in the blackest darkness.

> Proverbs, 20:20

Train up a child in the way he should go, and even when he is old, he will not depart from it.

> Proverbs, 22:6

A woman of valor who can find? For her price is far above rubies. The heart of her husband does safely trust in her. And he has not lack of gain. She does him good and not evil all the days of her life.

> Proverbs, 31:10-12

Like a father has compassion upon his children, so has the Lord compassion upon them that fear Him.

> Psalms, 103:13

Three bring the human being to life: God, his father, and his mother. When a human being honors father and mother, God says: I give him credit for this as if I would be honored by them. When a human being is bad to his father or mother, God says: I do right that I am not with him because if I were with him, he would be bad also toward Me.

> Bab. Talmud Kiddushin, 30B

When the blind Rabbi Jose heard his mother's footsteps, he said: I will rise up before God's holiness which reveals itself.

      Bab. Talmud Kiddushin, 31B

One shall never spread fear around himself in his house through too great strictness.

      Bab. Talmud Gittin, 6B

One shall never prefer one child to the other. Because of the colored cloak which Jacob gave to Joseph alone, his brothers became jealous and did things which led the father to worries and to Egypt.

      Bab. Talmud Shabbat, 10B

Ben Asai taught: Everyone is bound also to teach his daughters the Torah.

      Bab. Talmud Sota, 20A

One shall be very careful not to insult one's wife. Her tears come very easily and it is very easy to hurt her.

      Bab. Talmud Baba Metzia, 59A

If your wife is short, you shall bow down to her when you want to consult with her.

      Bab. Talmud Baba Metzia, 59A

He who loves his wife like himself and who honors her more than himself, of him it is said: "And thou shalt know that thy tent is in peace. And thou shalt visit thy habitation, and shalt miss nothing" (Job, 5:24).

      Bab. Talmud Jebamot, 62B

His home, that is his wife.

      Bab. Talmud Yoma, 2A

The honoring of father and mother is of such importance that God sets that higher than to honor Himself.

      Jer. Talmud Peah, 1:1

What is respect for father and mother and what is honor? Respect is that one does not sit on their seat, that one does not interrupt them when they talk and not insist to be right towards them.

Honoring is that one supply them with food and cloth,
when they need it, and do not let them work.

      Sifra to Leviticus, 19:3

A son shall clothe his parents better than himself.

      Tanna Debe Eliahu, 26

It was taught in Rabbi Meir's name: Between man and
wife rests God's holiness. When they show themselves
worthy of it, the divine holiness stands between them
and blessings rest over them. Are they unworthy, God's
holiness abandons them and a curse meets them.

      Midrash Lekach Tov to Genesis, 1

One shall always endeavour to teach his son Torah and
lead him to the right path. Those who do this, show
them the way and make them go it, will be greatly rewarded.

      Midrash Leolam, 11

THE INDIVIDUAL AND SOCIETY

Judaism does not know asceticism or monasticism. It has - in contrast to other religions - no place for pious people isolated from the world, who in seclusion or behind cloister walls, together with **brethren** or sisters, who have the same attitude, try to live a life pleasant to God. During the time of the Second Temple there were tendencies to such a flight from the world, and small assemblies of "Holies" were founded in the wilderness at the Dead Sea. They disappeared, however, quickly enough.

Judaism affirms the natural human society, the family and the community, which grows up at the side of the family, by fostering the family into an organization. It is positively focused on each other living community where the individual is respected and privileges and responsibilities are the same for all. Humanity's social connections are, according to Jewish tradition and teachings, not the lesser of two evil things. They are good in themselves, desirable and necessary. For only in these connections can the human being become to his fellow being a support and help, and thus document his love for responsibility and his solidarity. There is no human being, who for one or another reason, is not dependent on others. Justice, fairness, love and humbleness cannot be shown if we do not live together with human beings, among them and for them.

The religious spirit which holds together the Jewish home unites also the Jews to the same degree to a strong unity and sets its sign on the Jewish community. The community preserves the tradition of Judaism and takes the responsibility for the functioning of the religious and social institutions which it keeps alive. Every local community is completely independent and has the right to decide about its affairs. To support the work of the community and the unselfish labor for others within the community, goes in as a clear demand of Judaism's social ethics within its general principles.

The duty to live together with others stretches, however, beyond the borders of one's own community. The duties of the citizens are, in Judaism, religious duties. From the religious commandment arises also the social will which sees in every human being - independent of his or her nation, race or religion - a fellow human being, as witnessed by the adherence for the laws of the state and the prayer for its welfare. Beyond the religious and national unity gleams the classical prophet's eternal truth and vision for a time, when peoples will extend their hands in sincere peacefulness and mankind's unity will be established.

And Moses said unto Aaron: "This is it that the Lord spoke, saying: Through them that are near unto Me I will be sanctified, and before all the people I will be glorified."

> Leviticus, 10:3

And seek the welfare of the city to which I have exiled you and pray to the Lord in its behalf; for in its prosperity you shall prosper.

> Jeremiah, 29:7

And they that are wise shall shine as the brightness of the firmament. And they that turn the many to righteousness as the stars for ever and ever.

> Daniel, 12:3

Rabbin Gamliel, the son of Rabbi Juda the Prince, said: An excellent thing is the study of the Torah combined with some worldly occupation, for the labor demanded by them both, makes sin to be forgotten. All study of the Torah without work, must in the end be futile and become the cause of sin. Let all who are employed with the congregation act with them for heaven's sake, for then the merit of their fathers sustains them, and their righteousness endures for ever.

> Sayings of the Fathers, 2:2

Hillel said: Separate not thyself from the congregation.

> Sayings of the Fathers, 2:5

Samuel said: A human being shall never separate himself from the community.

> Bab. Talmud Berachot, 49B

Samuel said: The laws of the land are laws.

> Bab. Talmud **Baba** Kamma, 113A

The messenger of the King is like the King.

> Bab. Talmud Baba Kamma, 113B

Rabbi Juda said: He who opposes his kind opposes also God's glory.

> Midrash Bereshit Rabba, 94

You shall not accept a public office if you are not

qualified for it.

> Pesikta Rabbati to Exodus, 20:7

It is easy to ascend on the scene and hard to descend from it.

> Jalkut Shimoni Vaetchanan, 6

If the shepherd goes astray, the flock also goes in his path.

> Pirke Rabbi Elieser, 40

ISRAEL, THE CHOSEN PEOPLE

Judaism's faith also contains the concept that Israel's people have a special task in the history of mankind. God chose this people in an historic moment, at a time when it not yet existed as a nation. Abraham left his heathen Babylonic family to become the ancestor of this people. Of his sons one was chosen - Isaac - and of the latter's sons again one - Jacob - later also named Israel, was chosen, and from his children originate the chosen people. This people contributed decisively within the framework of the spiritual, ethical, moral and social history of the world.

Israel being chosen has its reason in God's love. Because God loved Israel He chose His people while they were still in bondage in the Land of Egypt. "The Lord did not set His love upon you, nor choose you, because ye were more in number than any people - for ye were the fewest of all peoples. But because the Lord loved you and because He would keep the oath which He swore unto your fathers, has the Lord brought you out of the house of bondage, from the hand of Pharaoh, King of Egypt." (Deuteronomy, 7:7-8). This love is mutual. Because Israel loved God, she made in her greatest historic event, the covenant at Sinai, in which she got the revelation of the Ten Commandments, an eternal compact between God and mankind. The mutuality of the love sealed Israel's choseness. A greater distinction than this choseness cannot be thought of. However, this is not a privilege. It is combined with obligations which must be fulfilled and duties which cannot be neglected, even if it means isolation and anxiety, suffering and death. Otherwise the choseness can turn to disaster: "You alone have I singled out of all the families of the earth - that is why I will call you to account for all your iniquities" (Amos, 3:2). Nor does choseness guarantee worldly bliss. Israel's choseness does not mean that Jews are better than other people. God is one God for all. Israel is God's "First Born", chosen among the people to serve God in truth and as the first to, completely and voluntarily, accept strict monotheism as their faith; thus chosen to be "God's servants" with more and additional commandments, duties and obligations. For the chosen people every righteous human being could be Israel. In the course of centuries and millenia pious, righteous, ethical and moral non-Jews could join the Jewish belief and people, if they wanted to profess the God of Israel. Every modern Jew is not only a descendant of his ancestors but also of the righteous proselytes who converted to Judaism. The Moabite woman Ruth became the ancestress of King David and thus an ancestress to the expected Messiah.

Now the Lord said to Abraham: "Get thee out of thy country, and from thy kindred, and from thy father's house, unto the land that I will show thee. And I will make of thee a great nation, and I will bless thee, and make thy name great: and be thou a blessing. And I will bless them that bless thee, and him that curseth thee will I curse. And in thee shall all the families of the earth be blessed."

Genesis, 12:1-3

And God appeared unto Jacob again, when he came from Paddan-Aram, and blessed him. And God said unto him: "Thy name is Jacob. Thy name shall not be called any more Jacob, but Israel shall be thy name." And He called his name Israel. And God said unto him: "I am God Almighty. Be fruitful and multiply. A nation and a company of nations shall be of thee, and kings shall come out of thy loins. And the land which I gave unto Abraham and Isaac, to thee I will give it, and to thy seed after thee will I give the land."

Genesis, 35:9-12

And ye shall be unto Me a kingdom of priests and a holy nation.

Exodus, 19:6

Thus said the Lord, who created the heavens and stretched them out, who spread out the earth and what it brings forth, who gave breath to the people upon it and life to those who walk thereon: I the Lord in My grace have summoned you, and I have grasped you by the hand. I created you, and appointed you a covenant people, a light of nations - opening eyes deprived of light, rescuing prisoners from confinement, from the dungeon those who sit in darkness.

Isaiah, 42:5-7

The people I formed for Myself that they might declare My praise.

Isaiah, 43:21

Indeed, My servant shall prosper, be exalted and raised to great heights. Just as the many were appalled at him - so marred was his appearance, unlike that of man, his form beyond human semblance - just so he shalt startle many nations. Kings shall be silenced because of him, for they shall see what has not been told them, shall behold what they never have heard.

> Isaiah, 52:13-15

You alone have I singled out of all the families of the earth - that is why I will call you to account for all your iniquities.

> Amos, 3:2

Said the Holy, praised be He, to Israel: I have made Me unique in the world and I make you unique in the world. I have made Me unique, as it is said: "Hear, O Israel, the Lord is One" (Deuteronomy, 6:4), and I make you unique, as it is said: "Who is like Thy people Israel, a nation one in the earth" (First Chronicles, 17:20).

> Bab. Talmud Berachot, 6A

This people is like dust and like the stars. If it falls it falls down to the dust and if it rises up it rises to the stars.

> Bab. Talmud Megilla, 16A

"And the souls that they (Abraham and Sarah) had made in Haran" (Genesis, 12:5). These are the converts which they had made. Understand from that that those who make converts are like they had brought them into the world.

> Midrash Bereshit Rabba, 99

The proselytes are loved because everytime the Torah equals them with Israel.

> Midrash Bamidbar Rabba, 8

Rabbi Akiba used to say: Beloved are Israel, for they were called children of the Allpresent. But it was by a special love that it was made known to them that they were called children of the Allpresent, as it is said: Ye are children, unto the Lord your God. (Deuteronomy, 14:1). Beloved are Israel, for unto them was given the desirable instrument. But it was by a special love that it was made known to them that that desirable instrument was theirs, through which the world was created. As it is said: For I give you good doctrine, forsake ye not my law. (Proverbs, 4:2).

Israel says: "As an apple-tree among the trees of the wood, so is my beloved among the sons." (Song of Songs, 2:3), and the Holy One says: "As a lily among thorns, so is my love among the daughters." (Song of Songs, 2:2).

Israel says: "This is my God, and I will glorify Him." (Exodus, 15:2), and the Holy One says: "The people I formed for Myself, that they might declare My praise." (Isaiah, 43:21).

Sifre to Deuteronomy, 33

Said Eliah, the prophet: I call heaven and earth as witnesses: May it be an Israelite or a gentile, a man or a woman, a slave or a slavemaid - all of them have the spirit of God in accordance with their deeds.

Tanna Debe Eliahu Rabba, 10

"Let thy priests be clothed with righteousness" (Psalms, 132:9). The righteous among the human beings on earth, these are the real priests to the Holy One, praised be He.

Tanna Debe Eliahu Sutta, 20

THE LAND OF ISRAEL

Israel is God's chosen people. It was chosen even before it existed by God's covenant with Abraham, the ancestor of the people. God determined a land for His chosen people, even before the people were there. God led Abraham into this land and to him promised He it and to his descendants, the people of Israel. Through the forefather Abraham, the Land of Canaan became Israel's "Fathers" land. Israel's right to this land rests upon God's promise. It is the Holy Land. Land and people have been determined for each other and are based on each other.

The people was not born in the land. It wandered into it, after the liberation from slavery in Egypt and a wandering of forty years through the wilderness. Born in the land was the pagan religion with its divination of nature. There was no greater danger which the classical prophets saw clearer, feared more and vigorously fought more, than that the people, when it became settled, should assimilate with the contemporary inhabitants, the Canaanites, and, like them should worship Baal and other nature gods and thus forget the high religious and ethical commandments which gave them the uniqueness among the peoples. The Canaanites had with their immorality not only defiled the land but also themselves. Because of that, the land was unworthy and God took it from them. The same fate threatened Israel if they defiled themselves and the land. They could again lose the land. And they did and were forced to leave it.

But the covenant initiated by God between the people and the land is an eternal covenant. It can be broken by the people but never dissolved. God always comes back to Zion. Zion, Jerusalem's fortress, which King David made his residence, stays as a symbol for the whole land. The people returning to Zion come not only to find themselves again, but come also in accordance with the word of the classical prophets: to be a light for the people. Zion's revival is the world's revival. Jerusalem becomes a new, united heart of humanity.

Judaism and the Jewish people have during the long centuries of diaspora always kept the conviction of its belonging to this promised land. The yearning to this land of Israel was a religious dream. With "Next Year In Jerusalem" finishes every year, wherever Jews live, the nocturnal celebration of the Seder, the celebration to commemorate the liberation from slavery in Egypt. The prayers for dew and rain are recited on Passover and at the end of the Sukkot holidays. They are said on these festivals because they fall at the time when the land of Israel is in need

of dew and rain. Reminders of Zion and Jerusalem appear again
and again in the daily and the festival prayers. For thousands
of years the Jewish people prayed three times daily for the restoration and rebuilding of Jerusalem. If possible, synagogues
are built towards the east (especially the Holy Ark). It should
point towards Jerusalem. The love for this tiny land has in all
times brought pilgrims from all the countries of the dispersion
and often, if possible, great waves of immigrants to the Holy
Land. This is a living witness and evidence that the land waits
for Jews. The dream that Judaism and the Jewish people is born
again in the promised land, has been fulfilled in our time and in
our generation. A great responsibility rests now on the Jewish
people. Every Jew, wherever he or she was born or lives, has the
responsibility that the people of Israel in the land of Israel
and the land of Israel through the people of Israel are what they
ought to be according to God's design and intention.

> And the Lord appeared unto Abram, and said: "Unto thy
> seed will I give this land." And he built there an
> altar unto the Lord, who appeared unto him.
>
> > Genesis, 12:7
>
> And I will give unto thee and to thy seed after thee,
> the land of thy sojournings, all the land of Canaan,
> for an everlasting possession. And I will be their God.
>
> > Genesis, 17:8
>
> And the land shall not be sold in perpetuity. For the
> land is Mine. For ye are strangers and settlers with Me.
>
> > Leviticus, 25:23
>
> For the Lord thy God bringeth thee into a good land,
> a land of brooks of water, of fountains and depths,
> springing forth in valleys and hills. A land of wheat
> and barley and vines and fig-trees and pomegranates,
> a land of olive trees and honey. A land wherein thou
> shalt eat bread without scarceness, thou shalt not
> lack any thing in it. A land whose stones are iron,
> and out of whose hills thou mayest dig brass. And thou
> shalt eat and be satisfied, and bless the Lord thy God
> for the good land which He has given thee.
>
> > Deuteronomy, 8:7-10
>
> The land, wither ye go over to possess it, is a land
> of hills and valleys, and drinketh water as the rain
> of heaven cometh down. A land which the Lord thy God
> careth for. The eyes of the Lord, thy God, are always

upon it, from the beginning of the year even unto the end of the year.

> Deuteronomy, 11:11-12

And there is hope for your future - declares the Lord: Your children shall return to their country.

> Jeremiah, 31:17

Thus said the Lord of Hosts, the God of Israel: They shall again say this in the land of Judah and in its towns when I restore their fortunes: "The Lord bless you, abode of righteousness, O holy mountain!" Judah and all its towns alike shall be inhabited by the farmers and such as move about with the flocks.

> Jeremiah, 31:23-25

Prophesy, therefore, and say to them: Thus said the Lord God: I am going to open your graves and lift you out of the graves, O My people, and bring you to the Land of Israel. You shall know, O My people, that I am the Lord when I have opened your graves and lifted you and you shall live again, and I will set you upon your own soil. Then you shall know that I the Lord have spoken and have acted - declares the Lord.

> Ezekiel, 37:12-14

If I forget thee, O Jerusalem, let my right hand forget her cunning. Let my tongue cleave to the roof of my mouth, if I remember thee not. If I set not Jerusalem above my chiefest joy.

> Psalms, 137:5-6

The Land of Israel is the holiest of all the lands.

> Mishna Kelim, 1:6

The air in the Land of Israel makes man wise.

> Bab. Talmud Baba Batra, 158B

Rami Bar Ezekiel came once to B'nai Brack and saw goats graze under a fig tree. Honey dripped from the figs and milk from the goats so that both blended. He said: "A land flowing with milk and honey." (Exodus, 3:8).

> Bab. Talmud Ketubot, 111B

Said Rabbi Joshua Ben Levi: "Jerusalem, thou art built as a city that is compact together." (Psalms, 122:3) - Jerusalem joins together the whole of Israel to a union.

> Jer. Talmud Chagiga, 3:6

Said Rabbi Seera: A child gets Torah with his mother-milk in the Land of Israel.

> Midrash Vajikra Rabba, 34

Said the Holy One, praised be He to Moses: I love the land and I love Israel. I will lead Israel whom I love into the land which I love.

> Midrash Bamidbar Rabba, 23

Rabbi Jochanan Ben Zakkai used to say: If you were busy to plant and somebody tells you that the Messiah has come, continue first your planting and then go out to welcome the Messiah.

> Abot de Rabbi Natan, 31

Ten measurements of beauty were given to the world - nine to Jerusalem and one for the rest of the world.

> Abot de Rabbi Natan, 48

THE HEBREW LANGUAGE

The Hebrew language is called in Judaism the Holy language. In this tongue Judaism possesses an instrument with the help of which it was, and is, able to express itself and its mental and spiritual life in a perfect manner. In this language God's word was revealed to mankind. Almost the whole Bible is written in Hebrew, a few parts are written in the Aramaic language which is closely related to Hebrew. Today, like from the beginning, the Jew approaches his God in Hebrew. What mankind deepest felt and knew and fairest dreamt, has never come so wonderfully expressed as in the Holy language, like in the Psalms, sung all over the world in Synagogues, Churches and Mosques. The Hebrew prayer book (the Siddur) contains pearls of the inward religious poetry originating from various times. In this tongue exults and grieves the Jewish soul, bends himself in fear and lifts himself in heavenly happiness. This language has been, and is, the living chain of association (connection) between Jew and Jew from the days of the Bible until our time. In this language Judaism has a rich literature and each century has contributed to the development of the language so that it, through creating new terms and words, always stayed a fresh, living, breathing tool in the service of humanity's cultural work, from biblical times until today. Because the Jew, wherever he lived, through Bible and prayer book, stood in loving contact with Hebrew, he always could in another country take part in the spiritual, cultural, and religious work of Judaism and Jews. Thus, the Hebrew language remained a living language, never untied from the life and soul of the Jewish people. Even when the Jews accepted the language of the environment, when they spoke Arabic or Spanish or German or Yiddish or English, the Hebrew tongue remained the means of expression for the Jewish community and its feelings of belonging to each other. Hebrew always exercised a strong influence on their daily, ordinary language.

Hebrew is, of course, the living and official language in the State of Israel. Poets, playwrights, authors, press, radio, television, art and politics are alive in the old-new tongue. It has adapted itself to all the modern thoughts and expressions and to modern life. It is, as it has been, the linguistic chain of connection between Jews who from all over the world come to Israel and take part as a link in this chain, between our time and all the epochs in the Jewish peoples past.

One can also speak profane things in the Holy language.

                    Bab. Talmud Shabbat, 41A

Said Rabbi Jehuda in the name of Rav: The inhabitants of the land Juda esteemed their language and the teaching remained with them. The inhabitants of the land Galilea did not esteem their language and the teaching did not remain with them.

                    Bab. Talmud Eruvin, 53A

"Come, let us go down, and there confound their language, that they may not understand one another's speech." (Genesis, 11:7). He confounded their language and nobody understood his comrade. In the beginning men and women spoke the Holy language and in it the universe was created. Said the Holy One, praised be He: In the world the evil instinct divides My creatures and they are separated into seventy tongues. But in the world to come they shall be united to serve Me as it is written: "For then I will make the peoples pure of speech, so that they all invoke the Lord by name and serve Him with one accord." (Zephania, 3:9).

                    Midrash Tanchuma Noah

"And thou shall teach them your children, talking of them, when thou sitteth in thy house, and when thou walkest by the way, and when thou liest down, and when thou risest up" (Deuteronomy, 11:19). Our sages say to this: When the child starts to speak, the parents shall talk to it the Holy language and teach it in that tongue.

                    Sifre Ekev

It was learned in the name of Rabbi Meir: He who dwells in the land of Israel and in the morning and evening recites his "Hear, O Israel" and speaks the Holy language, he can be sure of the coming world.

                    Sifre Haasinu

JUDAISM'S MAIN BOOKS

The main books written in Hebrew and Aramaic which contain Judaism's teachings, philosophy, rules, commandments and customs were imparted from one generation to the next. Every epoch has, by a new spiritual and mental creation, sought its own explanation and understanding of Judaism and thus commented upon the traditional scriptures and writings in its own way. Therefore, has the religious literature with "the people of the book" grown to an extraordinarily rich library which still keeps on growing. All the works around Judaism are built on the Bible, Judaism's creature and most precious jewel, yet also mankind's most important literary work.

THE BIBLE

   Bible is a Greek word that means "The Book". With that is meant the Book of Books, the Holy Scriptures which has been and is a force without comparison in Judaism's and mankind's history. The Jews denote the book with an artificial Hebrew memory word, Tenach, which contains the beginning letters of the names of the three main parts of the Bible: Torah (five books of Moses); Nevi'im (Prophets); Ketuvim (Holy Writings). The Christians call the early part of the Bible the Old Testament because they consider their New Testament as belonging to the Bible.

   The Bible is the most translated book in world literature. Of the old translations the following are the most important:

   TARGUMIN, in singular Targum, the Aramaic Jewish Bible translations of which the most important are the Aramaic translations of the Torah, the **so called Targum Onkelos.**

   SEPTUAGINT, a Greek translation, that was done in Egypt on Jewish initiative at the beginning of our time table. According to a legend, seventy men did independently this translation which came out in conformity. Therefore, it was called Septuagint, 70.

   PESHITTA, the Syrian translation.

   VULGATA, the Christian Church Father Hieronymus' (340-420) Latin translation.

   The SAMARITAN translation which only contains the Five books of Moses and the book of Joshuah.

   According to the Jewish division, the Bible is composed of 24 books in three parts:

   I. The TORAH is called with a Greek expression PENTATEUCH and with another Hebrew word CHUMASH. Both mean Five-Book, meaning the Five Books of Moses. The diverse books are called:

       1. The First Book of Moses, in Hebrew BERESHIT, in Greek GENESIS (Beginning). The content is the creation of the world, the history of the ancestors of the people of Israel until their immigration to Egypt.

2. The Second Book of Moses, in Hebrew SHEMOT (names), in Greek-Latin EXODUS (exodus from Egypt). It tells of the exodus from the slavery in Egypt to freedom and the revelation at Sinai. It contains many commandments and gives a description of the tabernacle to be erected in the desert.

3. The Third Book of Moses, in Hebrew, VAJIKRA (He called), in Latin, LEVITICUS (the priestly laws). This book contains laws concerning the sacrifices, priestly laws, ethical and moral laws.

4. The Fourth Book of Moses, in Hebrew, BAMIDBAR (in the desert), in Latin, NUMERI (numbers). The book starts with a census in the desert and tells of the problems and events of the long wanderings in the desert.

5. The Fifth Book of Moses, in Hebrew, DEVARIM (the words), in Greek-Latin, DEUTERONOMY (Repetition of Law). Its contents are Moses' great farewell address in which many many commandments (and again the Ten Commandments) are interlaced. It ends with the narration of Moses' death.

II. The Books of the Prophets, in Hebrew, NEVIIM. The so-called "First Prophets" are historic books which give account of the history of the people, from the time when they entered the promised land, until the Babylonian exile. The "Later Prophets" are composed of various prophetic stories.

  A. The First Prophets:

   1. THE BOOK OF JOSHUAH. It reports of the conquest and the taking possession of the land and its distribution among the tribes.

   2. THE BOOK OF JUDGES, in Hebrew, SHOFTIM. It relates of the time when Israel was led by godly inspired heroes, called Judges, who were not always divinely inspired and who lacked the capacity and the vision of a united people and a nation true to its faith and mission in the world.

   3. THE TWO SAMUEL BOOKS, in Hebrew, SHMUEL (Samuel), tell of the prophet Samuel, his work and achievements as the last Judge and the life and deeds of the first two kings of Israel, Saul and David.

4. THE TWO BOOKS OF KINGS, in Hebrew, MELACHIM. They begin with King Solomon's accession to the throne through his reign, describe the partition of the kingdom in the southern state of Judah (with the capital of Jerusalem) and the northern state of Israel (with the capital of Samaria) and the destruction of the two kingdoms. In these two books we also find the tales of the prophets Elia and Elisha.

A. The Later Prophets.

These are arranged according to the size of the books so that the three biggest "Great" prophets, Isaiah, Jeremiah, and Ezekiel come first and the twelve "small prophets" follow, collected in one book.

1. ISAIAH. He worked from 750 until 700 B.C.E. To this book is annexed the so-called "Second Isaiah", an unknown prophet in the Babylonian exile.

2. JEREMIAH. He worked from 627 until after 586 B.C.E. and was a contemporary at the destruction of Jerusalem and the First Temple by the Babylonians.

3. EZEKIEL. He worked in the Babylonian exile, around 575 B.C.E.

4. The Small Prophets:

Hoseah; Joel; Amos; Obadjah; Jonah; Micah; Nachum; Habakkuk; Zephanjah; Haggai; Zecharjah; Malachi. These prophets worked at diverse times. Amos belongs to the first writing prophets (around 780 B.C.E.). The three last prophets lived after the Babylonian captivity. (Around 520 B.C.E.)

III. The other holy books are called in Hebrew: KETUVIM, in Greek: HAGIOGRAPHA.

1. PSALMS, in Hebrew: TEHILLIM. The biggest part of the religious songs collected in this book and sung in all places of worship of the monotheistic faiths is, according to tradition, believed to originate from King David. The psalms belong to the master works in poetry in world literature.

2. PROVERBS, in Hebrew: MISHLE. A wisdom book, in tradition attributed to King Solomon.

3. THE BOOK OF JOB. The story of the suffering of Job discussing with his friends God's justice.

4. THE SONG OF SONGS, in Hebrew: SHIR HASHIRIM. A collection of love songs which is attributed to King Solomon and which, according to traditions, sing of the relation between God and Israel, His chosen people. This book is read at Passover.

5. THE BOOK OF RUTH. The story of the Moabite woman Ruth who converted to Judaism and became the ancestress of King David. The book is read at Shavuot, the Festival of the Weeks.

6. JEREMIAH'S LAMENTATIONS, in Hebrew: ECHA. Lamentations about the destruction of the Holy Temple in Jerusalem. This book is read at the ninth of Av.

7. ECCLESIASTES, in Hebrew: KOHELET. A book with a rather pessimistic brand of wisdom, view of life and philosophy, attributed according to tradition, to King Solomon. The book is read at the Sabbath of the Festival of the Tabernacles, Sukkot.

8. THE BOOK OF ESTHER. The story of Purim. This book is read at the Festival of Purim.

9. THE BOOK OF DANIEL. It tells of the experiences of Daniel and his friends and also contains Daniel's prophecies.

10. THE BOOKS OF EZRA AND NEHEMIA. The story of the return from the Babylonian exile and of the newly established Jewish commonwealth.

11. THE TWO BOOKS OF THE CHRONICLES, in Hebrew: DIVRE HAYAMIM. They tell once more the history of Israel.

Many books which in spite of their very valuable religious contents were not included into the Holy Scripture's Canon, are called Apocrypha (Hidden Writings). Among the most important of those books which are mostly reserved in Greek, are the Books of the Maccabees, the Book of Judit and Ecclesiasticus (The Book of Wisdom of Joshua ben Sira) of which we also have the Hebrew original text.

THE ORAL LAW

In contrast to the Bible, which was available already in early times in written form, stands the so-called Oral Law. It consists of an extended literature, which kept on growing for centuries. Its aim has been to put in order the biblical commandments and rules, and through explanations and commentaries to adapt them to the reality of life. Many of the commandments of the Torah suppose old oral traditions that explain these commands. Such traditions could, certainly, go back to the times of the Babylonian captivity. The reason that they were not put into writing was that there really was only one written book: the Bible. Not before these traditions swelled into an extent that made it impossible to keep it longer in an oral form was the oral law written down and likewise the oral tradition, which is a collection of writings that, in the course of time, got considerable enlargement. The oral law's most important part which is given to the legal side of Judaism and embraces personal, social, national, religious, international and all other practices and observances of Judaism is called HALACHAH, meaning: The way to go. In contrast to the Halachah there is the AGGADAH, meaning: The Narrative Part of the Oral Law. Aggadah is a collective conception for that part of the Oral Law which is not concerned with religious laws and regulations. It is for the most part an amplification of those portions of the Bible which include narrative, history, ethical maxims, the reproofs and consolations of the prophets, legends, explanations of texts in sermon forms and theological dogma.

A collection of commentaries and explanations to books of the Bible or to old traditions is called MIDRASH or in plural MIDRASHIM, meaning: Research, investigating. It is an anthology and compilation of homilies, consisting of both biblical exegesis and sermons delivered in public. The Midrash forms a running commentary on specific books of the Bible. There are halachic and aggadic Midrashim dependent upon their content.

The First Book of the Torah, Bereshit (Genesis), has almost no religious regulations and therefore there is no halachic Midrash on this book. The halachic Midrash on the second book is called Mechilta, meaning: Measure, Norm. On the third book it is Sifra (Book), and on the fourth and fifth books of Moses it is Sifre (Books).

There are Aggadic Midrashim from the various epoches mainly on the five books of Moses and the five "Scrolls": Song of Songs, Ruth, Lamentations, Ecclestiastes and Esther. These Midrashim are called Midrash Rabba meaning: The Big Midrash. When, therefore, in this book something is quoted from MIDRASH BERESHIT RABBA or from MIDRASH SHIR HASHIRIM RABBA, it refers to the "great" Midrashim on the First Book of Moses or on the Song of Songs. Two types of Midrashim can be distinguished: the exegetical and the homiletical. The exegetical (like Genesis Rabba, Song of Songs Rabba, Lamentations Rabba, et. al.) is a Midrash to one of the books of the Bible, containing comments on the whole book, on each chapter, on every verse, and, at times, even on every word in the verse. The homiletical Midrash is either a Midrash to a book of the Pentateuch in which only the first verse (or verses) of the weekly portion if expounded or a Midrash that is based only on the biblical and prophetic reading of special Sabbaths and Festivals in which also the first verses are expounded (e.g., PIRKEI DE RAV KAHANA and PESIKTA [Section], RABBATI [Great Section]). In contrast to the exegetical Midrashim, the homiletical Midrashim contain almost no short homilies on variegrated topics, but each chapter (or section) constitutes a collection of homilies and sayings on one topic that seem to combine into one long homily on the specific topic.

There are also shorter Midrashim collected into anthologies, the most famous among them is JALKUT SHIMONI, meaning: Simon's Knapsack. Most of the anthologies quote their sources with their original wording. The Midrash literature expands until the Middle Age period.

Originally, the Oral Law meant as a general designation the MISHNAH, (Repetition, Learning). There are six orders (SEDARIM) of the Mishnah that were redacted, arranged, and revised about the beginning of the third century by Rabbi Jehuda Ha-Nassi, who was known simply as Rabbi. The Mishnah is the canonized collection of Judaism's laws and commands which, however, is not, like the halachic Midrashim, arranged after the various books of the Torah but systematically after relevant principles. The Mishnah is the official commentary on the laws of the Bible. The word was used specifically to designate the HALACHAH (the Law) for which it became a synonym. It is divided into the orders ZERAIM (seeds), MOED (festivals), NASHIM (women), NEZIKIN (damages), KODASHIM (holy things), TOHOROT (purities). The six main parts or orders are divided in 63 tractates, each tractate in various sections and each section in various paragraphs which, like the whole work, also is called Mishnah. The first of the six orders, ZERAIM (seeds), begins with a tractate dealing with prayers and blessings and, besides, contains other tractates which treat of the regulations concerning agriculture. The second order, MOED (festivals), contains the tractates concerning the Sabbath, festivals and fastdays. The third order, NASHIM (women) deals with the marriage laws. The fourth order, NEZIKIN (damages), includes the whole civil and criminal law and, besides, has a supplement called PIRKEI AVOT (Sayings of the Fathers). It is the most widely known of all the 63 tractates of the Mishnah. It is unique in character. The Mishnah is a code of laws governing Jewish life. But this tractate is almost entirely concerned with ethical conduct. It furnishes teachings of what the Jewish sages considered fundamental aspects of life. A parallel collection to it is the so-called AVOT DE RABBI NATHAN (Sayings of Rabbi Nathan). The fifth order KODASHIM (holy things) speaks of the laws referring to the sacrifices in the Temple in Jerusalem and the sixth, TOHOROT (purities) has the regulations for cleanliness. The language of the Mishnah is Hebrew, a concise, beautiful Hebrew, yet not the pure Biblical Hebrew. Aramaic, Greek and Latin words are mixed in. When in this book, for example, the tenth section from the Mishnah for the Pessach (Passover) Festival is quoted, it is designated with: Mishnah Pessachim 10.

Besides the Mishnah there is another collection of religious laws (HALACHOT), arranged according to the order of the Mishnah, which is called TOSEFTA (Addition). With few exceptions, each tractate of the Mishnah has its parallel in the Tosefta. However, the Tosefta is about four times larger than the Mishnah. Like the Mishnah, the Tosefta is written in Hebrew, with very little Aramaic. However, the Mishnah is regarded as authoritative and forms the basis for the Babylonian and Palestinian TALMUD (Study, Learning). The word refers to the opinions and teachings which disciples acquire from their predecessors in order to expound and explain them. The word is, however, most commonly used to denote the body of teaching which comprises the commentary and discussions around the Mishnah and its meaning, led in the tongue of the people, Aramaic, tried once more to adapt the Jewish law and religion to the necessity of the time. These long discussions which sometimes are interrupted by stories and aggadic tales, are called GEMARAH (Completion; Tradition). In popular parlance, the two phrases of Mishnah and Gemarah together form the Talmud. The Talmud which has been edited in Palestine is shorter and older than the more extensive Babylonian, which is essentially the interpretation and elaboration of the Mishnah, as it was carried on in the great academies of Babylon. It was concluded around the year 500 A.D. In principal, the Talmud is also divided according to the same order as the Mishnah. It also accepted the popular name SHAS, an abbreviation consisting of the initial letters of SHIsha SIdrei (The Six Orders of the Mishnah).

While there are two Talmuds - the Babylonian and the Palestinian or the Jerusalem - the former, almost immediately upon its conclusion, was accepted as the authoritative one. It was studied assiduously in all the communities, while the Jerusalem Talmud was neglected. Undoubtedly, this is partly due to the difference between them in style and structure. The Babylonian is intellectually more interesting. The discussions are sharper and more sophisticated. The style is more lively, and the development of the themes is richer and stretches over a longer period. All this has made the Babylonian Talmud a more challenging and more exciting study. The general principle is, that, whenever the Jerusalem Talmud contradicts the Babylonian, the authority of the latter prevails. The text of the Talmud consists of some two and one half million words on 5,894 folio pages. About one third is Halachah and two thirds Aggadah. The Babylonian Talmud reflects about the daily life of the people. It is a storehouse of information connected with the life, customs, beliefs and superstitions of Jews and non-Jews. It is a source for history, medicine, astronomy, commerce, agriculture, demonology, botany, zoology and other sciences. It also contains homiletical exegesis of the Bible, moral maxims, popular proverbs, prayers, parables, fables, tales, accounts of manners and customs, Jewish and non-Jewish, Jewish and heathen folklore. It is virtually impossible to exaggerate the dominant position held by the Babylonian Talmud among Jews throughout the ages. Certainly from the time of Rashi (Solomon ben Isaac, 1040-1105), whose brilliant and indispensible commentary unlocked the secrets of its difficult language, until the advent of the 18th century, it was practically the sole subject of general Jewish education. To study "the sea of Talmud", so-called because of the multiplicity of its subjects, was continued throughout life.

The first printing of the Talmud came out in Venice, Italy in 1520-1523. All later editions accepted the page numbers of the first printing. Thus, if we quote, for example, "Bab. Talmud Berachot 16B" it means, that in any edition and printing, this quotation will be found in the tractate of Berachot (Blessings) on page 16 on the second side. On each side of the Talmud are commentaries. On the inside of the text is a commentary by Rabbi Solomon ben Isaac from Troyes, France who, under the abbreviated name of Rashi (1040-1105), became renown as the greatest and classical commentator of the Bible and Talmud. In the outer side of the text are some small commentaries called TOSSAFOT (Additions), explanations which French and German Talmud scholars gave from 1200 and later. Talmud commentaries were given already before Rashi and they represent a rich and vast literature within the literature of Judaism.

The Central European scholars had the goal to explain the Talmud. Moses Ben Maimon, called Maimonides, born in Cordova, Spain, 1135, died in Cairo, Egypt, 1204, made it his aim to classify by subject matter the entire Talmudic and post-Talmudic halachic literature in a systematic manner, never before attempted in the history of Judaism. He accomplished it in his work MISHNE TORAH (Repetition of the Law) or YAD HA-CHASAKAH (The Strong Hand), which was divided into fourteen books, each representing a distinct category of the Jewish legal system. (In Hebrew fourteen is Yad and hence the alternative name of the work Yad Ha-Chasakah, the strong hand). The Mishne Torah was written in a beautiful and lucid Hebrew, the like of which has not been known in halachic literature since the writing of the Mishnah. This book influenced the language of later codes. In this book he also shows with every biblical command the explanation and practical decision of the later oral law. Maimonides' systematization of the Talmud, in its entire structure, form and arrangement, was a cultural and historical phenomenon, a revolution, unprecedented in Jewish dogmatic jurisprudence, which both awed and shocked the scholarly world for centuries.

Other scholars with their systems followed the example of Maimonides. The last great systematic collection of all the commandments in Judaism was written by Rabbi Joseph Caro (1488-1575) who lived in Safed, Palestine and whose main work is: SHULCHAN ARUCH (The Prepared Table). The book ultimately became accepted as the code of Jewish law par excellence after amendments had been added by Rabbi Moses Isserles. With the commentaries, the Shulchan Aruch became the final authority to which one turned for the definite Halachah.

The halachic literature had been by the times immense. With this literature which existed up to then, Caro put together in a concise form the current laws and the excepted customs into a practical, short manual according to which the religious Jew can arrange his life.

JEWISH PHILOSOPHY AND MYSTICISM

Jewish philosophy may be described as the explanation of Jewish beliefs and practices by means of general philosophic concepts and norms. It can be seen as an outgrowth of the biblical and halachic traditions on which Judaism rests. Yet, the biblical and halachic traditions were indigenous products of the Jewish community. Jewish philosophy arose and flourished as Jews participated in the philosophic speculations of the external culture. Jewish philosophy deals with such topics as the election of Israel, the revelation, content, and eternity of the Torah; the special character of the prophecy of Moses; the Jewish conception of the Messiah and the afterlife. As philosophy of religion, it investigates issues common to Judaism, Christianity and Islam, such as the existence of God, divine attributes, the creation of the world, the phenomenon of prophecy, the human soul, and general principles of human conduct. It studies topics of general philosophic interest, such as the logical categories, the structure of logical arguments, the division of being, the nature and composition of the universe.

The Jewish philosophy of religion is rooted in the Bible and the rabbinic writings. It endeavors to bring religion and philosophy in agreement with each other. It emphasized always Judaism's ethical attitude and attempts to justify Judaism's religious laws. Of special interest were the more philosophical books of the Bible, including Proverbs, Job, Song of Songs, and Ecclesiastes, on which numerous philosophical commentaries were written.

PHILO OF ALEXANDRIA, (c. 20 B.C.E. - 50 C.E.) presented his views in a series of commentaries and passages of the Pentateuch, works on biblical topics, and independent philosophic treatises. He was influenced largely by Platonic and Stoic ideas, and his philosophy also has a mystical streak. His philosophy has been interpreted in several ways. But whatever interpretation one accepts, he is the founder of religious philosophy in Judaism, Christianity and Islam. Philo influenced the teachings of Church Fathers such as Clement of Alexandria, Origen, and Gregory of Nysea.

The first systematic Jewish philosopher of religion in the Middle Ages was SAADIAH (Ben Joseph) GAON (882-942), head of the rabbinical academy of Sura (near Baghdad). Influenced by the Arabic philosophy of religion, the Mutazilites, and relying on Platonic, Aristotelian and Stoic notions, he undertook to formulate a Jewish philosophy of religion. His major philosophic work divided into a section on divine unity and a section on divine justice is called: EMUNOT VEDEOT (Beliefs and Opinions). Saadiah in his book did not attempt to establish a complete philosophical system resting on an independent foundation. He rather set out to find rational proof for the teachings of the Written and Oral Law. Saadiah explains that he wrote his work in order to provide his fellow Jews with spiritual guidance in the face of the confusion which the multiple sects and religious disputes had created among people, and to combat heretical views. He believed that it was a religious obligation to provide a rational basis for the Law, in order to dispel doubts and refute views at variance with those which he accepts. His importance lies in his being the first medieval Jewish philosopher to attempt to reconcile the Bible and philosophy, reason and revelation. As in most of the Jewish philosophy of religion, in the center is the endeavor to philosophically explain the concept of God.

Toward the end of the 11th century BACHYA BEN JOSEPH IBN PAQUDA wrote his book: CHOVOT HA-LEVAVOT (Duties of the Hearts), a devotional manual which achieved great popularity among Jews. His work rests on a distinction between "duties of the limbs" religious commandments that require overt actions and "duties of the heart" those commandments which require specific beliefs and inner states (intentions). He holds that the latter are commanded by the Torah no less than the former. The final goal of all commandments is the love of God which Bachya defines as the soul's turning to God.

The most important Jewish Neoplatonist was SOLOMON BEN JUDAH IBN GABIROL (1020-1070). Beginning with him the setting of Jewish philosophy shifted to Spain. Also an important Hebrew poet, Ibn Gabirol presented his philosophy in his work: MEKOR CHAYIM (The Source of Life). The work is a pure philosophic treatise lacking biblical and rabbinic citations. It was widely circulated in Christian scholastic circles and its author was known under the name Avicebron. The goal to which all men should aspire is defined in the book as knowledge of the purpose for which they were created, that is, knowledge of the divine world. This knowledge brings release from death and attachment to "the source of life."

JEHUDAH HALEVI (before 1075-1141), ranking with Ibn Gabirol as one of the two most important Hebrew poets of the Middle Ages, wrote a philosophic work which is known under the title SEFER HA-KUZARI (The Book of the Kuzari). In it, he is critical of Aristotelian rationalism. In his time Aristotelianism was important in Islamic philosophy but not yet in Jewish religious philosophy. For him, historical experience, rather than physical and metaphysical speculations, is the source of truth, and religious practices are more important than beliefs and dogmas. The book is called The Kuzari after the Kings of the Khazars whose conversion to Judaism provides the literary framework. This literary framework enables Halevi to compare the teachings of Judaism with those of Aristotelianism, Islam and Christianity, in an effort to prove the superiority of Judaism. **Jehudah Halevi's views emerge in a** dialogue between the King and the Chaver, a Jewish scholar, who acts as the author's spokesman.

MOSES BEN MAIMON, called MAIMONIDES (1135-1204), whom we already mentioned, was the most illustrious figure in Judaism in the post-Talmudic era and one of the greatest of all time. He is the most prominent figure of medieval Jewish thought. Maimonides discusses his philosophy in popular fashion in parts of his halachic works, his commentary on the **Mishnah** and Mishne Torah (Repetition of the Torah) and in other treatises. But his book MOREH NEVUCHIM (Guide of the Perplexed) is the most important philosophic work produced by a Jew. In his philosophic views Maimonides was an Aristotelian and it was he who put medieval Jewish philosophy on a firm Aristotelian basis. Fundamental to Maimonides' approach is a division of mankind into two groups: an intellectual elite, who, using reason, can understand by means of demonstrative arguments, and the masses, including those scholars who study only religious law, who, using imagination, understand by means of persuasive arguments. In the light of this distinction Maimonides' works may be divided into two kinds: Guide of the Perplexed addressed primarily to an intellectual elite, and his other writings, addressed to the masses.

Maimonides wrote his Guide for someone who was firm in his religious beliefs and practices, but, having studied philosophy, was perplexed by the literal meaning of biblical anthropomorphic terms. To this person Maimonides showed that these difficulties have a spiritual meaning besides their literal one, and that it is the spiritual meaning that applies to God. Maimonides also undertook in the Guide the explanation of obscure biblical parables. Thus, the Guide is devoted to the philosophic interpretation of Scripture, or, to use Maimonides' terms, to the "science of the Law in its true sense" or to the "secrets of the Law" (Guide, Introduction). Maimonides' intellectualism is reflected in the formulation of 13 principles that in his view every member of the Jewish community is bound to accept.

Maimonides' Guide profoundly influenced the subsequent course of medieval Jewish religious philosophy. In addition to that, the Guide also had a formative influence on modern Jewish thought. Maimonides provided a first acquaintance with philosophic speculation for a number of philosophers of the Enlightenment period and served as a bridge for the study of more modern philosophy. Moses Mendelssohn is a case in point. In addition, Maimonides became a symbol for their own philosophic endeavors. He had attempted to introduce the spirit of rationalism into Jewish teachings during medieval times, just as they tried to do in their own time. Maimonides exercised an extensive influence on Christian scholastic thought. Among these scholastics are: Alexander of Hales; William of Auvergne; Albertus Magnus; Thomas Acquinas; Meister

Eckhart and Duns Scotus.

The influence of Maimonides on the future development of Judaism is incalculable. No spiritual leader of the Jewish people in the post-Talmudic period has exercised such an influence, both in his own and subsequent generations. Despite the vehement opposition which greeted his philosophical views, the breach was healed. It was probably due to his unrivaled eminence as talmudist and codifier that many of his views were finally accepted. They were very radical at the time. For instance, the now universally accepted doctrine of the incorporeality of God was by no means accepted as fundamental before him. Maimonides united the various currents of Judaism, the halachic and the philosophic, by showing in his Guide and the other works that there is no contradiction between faith and philosophy.

KABBALAH (Something handed down by Tradition) is the traditional and most commonly used term for the esoteric teachings of Judaism and for Jewish mysticism. In its wider sense, it signifies all the successive mystical movements in Judaism that evolved from the end of the period of the Second Temple and became active factors in the Jewish history.

Kabbalah is a unique phenomenon. It is mysticism. But, at the same time, it is also esotericism and theosophy. Kabbalah is mysticism as it seeks an apprehension of God and creation whose intrinsic elements are beyond the grasp of the intellect. These elements were perceived through contemplation and illumination, which is often presented in the Kabbalah as the transmission of a primeval revelation concerning the nature of the Torah and other religious matters. In essence, mysticism is far removed from the rational and intellectual approach to religion. This was the case even among those mystics who thought that basically religion was subject to rational inquiry. For some mystics the intellect itself became a mystical phenomenon. There are elements common to Kabbalah, the Jewish mysticism and both Greek and Christian mysticism. There are even historical links between them.

Like other kinds of mysticism, Jewish mysticism draws upon the mystic's awareness of both the transcendence of God and His eminence within the true religious life, every facet of which is a revelation of God. God Himself is most clearly perceived through man's introspection. This dual and apparently contradictory experience of the self-concealing and self-revealing God determines the essential sphere of mysticism, while at the same time it obstructs other religious conceptions. Jewish mysticism also seeks to reveal the mysteries of the hidden life of God and the relationships between the divine life on the one hand and the life of man and creation on the other. Speculations of this type occupy a large area in the teachings of Jewish mysticism. Mysticism is knowledge that cannot be communicated directly but may be expressed only through symbol and metaphor.

Many Kabbalists saw Jewish mysticism as a kind of primordial revelation that was accorded to Adam or the early generations and that endured, although new revelations were made from time to time, particularly when the tradition had been either forgotten or interrupted. This was expressed in apocryphal works like the Book of Enoch and was again stressed in the ZOHAR (The Book of Splendor).

Once rabbinic Judaism had crystallized in the Halachah, the forces of Jewish mysticism worked internally, attempting to make of the traditional Torah and of the life led according to its dictates, a more profound inner experience. The general tendency was to broaden the dimensions of the Torah and to transform it from the law of the people of Israel into the inner secret law of the universe. At the same time transforming the Jewish CHASSID or ZADDIK (Righteous man) into a man with a vital role in the world. For Jewish mysticism, Judaism, in all its aspects, was a system of mystical symbols, reflecting the mystery of God and the universe. The mystic's aim was to discover and invent keys to the understanding of this symbolism. To this aim is due the enormous influence of Jewish mysticiem as a historical force, which determined the face of Judaism for many centuries. It also explains the perils, upheavals and contradictions, internal and external, which the realization of this aim brought in its wake.

The main influence of Jewish mysticism on Jewish life must be sought in the three areas of prayer, custom and ethics. Here the Kabbalah had practically unlimited freedom to exert its influence, which expressed itself in the creation of a broad body of literature that was directed at every Jewish home. From the middle of the 17th century onward, Kabbalistic motifs entered the everyday prayer book and inspired special liturgies intended for a variety of specific occasions and rituals. Throughout the Diaspora, the number of folk-customs whose origins were Kabbalistic was enormous. Many were taken directly from the Zohar, the most important work for the stirring of a mythical spirit in medieval Judaism. This book is the Bible of Jewish mysticism.

The profoundly altered approach to Jewish history that followed in the wake of the Zionist revival, the movement for national rebirth and the establishment of the State of Israel led to a renewal of interest in Jewish mysticism as a vital expression of Jewish existence. A new attempt was made to understand, independently of all polemic or apologetic positions, the genesis, development, historical role, and social and intellectual influence of Jewish mysticism within the total context of the internal and external forces that have determined the shape of Jewish history. With the development of new perspectives in our times, scholarly investigation is only now emerging from its infancy.

    A religious movement which was born in Eastern Europe in the 18th century, the Chassidim, was nearer to Jewish mysticism than to the narrow intellectualism. Chassidism was not a completely new form of Judaism. It was a renewal movement. Its simple principles were: Joy of Living; Love of God and Man; Service to God and Man; Enthusiasm and Dedication to the Work of God. In the Chassidic philosophy the simplest human being could get as near to the Lord as the greatest scholar in his studies. Mystically, the Chassidic movement brought often comfort, courage, and a new will of life to these suffering stepchildren of humanity. Chassidism became, for those who joined this movement in Judaism, more than a collection of ideals and noble purposes. It became a way of life, in which the study of the Torah, prayer, good deeds and other religious duties must be carried out in love and devotion. The Holy Man, the Zaddik, the leader, has his thoughts constantly on God. He performs a double task: He brings man nearer to God and he brings down God's message and blessing to man. Chassidism counted among its adherents several of the leading Kabbalists.

MANY SHADES - ONE JUDAISM

ORTHODOXY-TRADITIONALIST

The term "Orthodoxy" as a reference within Judaism, first appeared in 1795, and became widely used from the beginning of the 19th century in contra-distinction to its reform movement. Orthodox came to designate those who accept as divinely inspired the totality of the historical religion of the Jewish people as it is recorded in the Written and Oral Laws and codified in the Shulchan Aruch and its commentaries until recent times. And as it is observed in practice according to the teachings and unchanging principles of the Halachah. Those who opposed changes and innovations in Jewish society and trends towards secularization felt it necessary to emphasize their stand as guardians of the Torah and its commandments under altered conditions and to find ways to safeguard their particular way of life.

Orthodox traditional Judaism considers itself the authentic bearer of the religious Jewish tradition which, until Emancipation, ruled over almost the entire Jewish community. Orthodoxy stresses the submission to the authority of the Halachah. Orthodoxy looks upon attempts to adjust Judaism to the spirit of the time as utterly incompatible with the entire thrust of the normative Judaism which holds that the revealed will of God rather than the values of any given age are the ultimate standard. In general, Orthodoxy is an all-out effort to preserve the status quo. Tampering with tradition was opposed.

Most orthodox authorities regard the Halachah **as a** body of rules handed down by God to enable the Jew to live according to His will. Some of these rules were transmitted by Moses in writing. Others were transmitted orally by him. Disobedience to some of the rules may be punished by authorities to whom God delegated that power. For other breaches of the Covenant He reserved unto Himself the power to punish.

In such a conception of the religion, man simply lives to obey the rules - and in obedience lies his salvation. To the extent that creativity is possible, it must be without reference to social or economic conditions, unless such considerations are implicit in the rule. Such instances are very few. The process of Halacha**h is** discovering what God had said. This is what the law is. Such an analysis must be strictly logical, arrived at, deductively or inductively, from existing rules and texts, without reference to ideal ends or social facts.

Thus, when in modern times the question arose as to whether light produced by an electric current does or does not constitute fire, and consequently whether it falls under the biblical prohibition on making fire on Sabbath, the approach of many who replied was purely analytical. The words and the applicable rules were carefully studied on the basis of textual distinction between hot coals and hot metals. The philosophical rationale of the biblical command was not relevant to the issue.

Persons unfamiliar with halachic literature often wonder, how there can be so many different Orthodox views when the analytical approach enjoys such overwhelming support. After all, if logic, rather than history and experience, is the life of the Halachah, can logic yield so many contradictory answers to the same question? Moreover, they question whether a revealed religion can ever evolve. Given that God's will is timeless and eternal, can man arrogate to himself the right to change it?

In general, a negative is assumed to be the correct reply to such questions. As a result, many Jews have come to regard Orthodox or Traditional Judaism as monolithic - as having a fixed philosophy, and a completely inflexible approach based on Jewish Law. The very term "Orthodox" conjures up the image of a central authority, comparable to that of the Pope, who makes ultimate decisions binding upon the faithful. This is, however, not even true of Roman Catholicism, and far less so of Orthodox Judaism. There have always been, and still are, different modes of Orthodox Jewish thought and practice. Traditionalism has always admitted a great measure of innovation. It is a fact that Orthodox Judaism has more splinter rabbinic groups than either Conservative or Reform Judaism. While Conservative and Reform rabbis are predominantly American, Orthodox Judaism has substantial rabbinic groups all over the world. Their number and diversity often reflect ideological as well as national and geographical differences. Members of these groups infrequently espouse ideas that are not typical for the particular groups to which they belong.

Not all Orthodox and Traditional Jews think alike or act alike. Orthodox rabbinic seminaries disagree as to the propriety of studying non-Jewish culture. New York's Rabbi Isaac Elchanan Theological Seminary, by far the largest, advocates the mastering of all Western thought in order to create an ultimate synthesis with Jewish learning. It was with this aim in mind that it founded Yeshiva University. Others hold that secular studies endanger faith. Others simply forbid their students to study anything other than Torah. This is the position of most Yeshivot in Israel. In the United States, one large group of Orthodox rabbis now cooperates with their Conservative and Reform colleagues in whatever areas their programs are similar. Others even refuse to address them as "rabbi".

The term Halachah is generally used to describe the literature of Jewish law, in distinction to the Aggadah which comprises the non-legal literature of Judaism. Yet, in fact, Jewish law comprises much more than is generally deemed law by modern states. It is important to bear this in mind when trying to understand, why there is so much diversity of rules and why there are so many different approaches to its development, even among those fervently committed to it. In modern states one of the most important characteristics of a law is its enforceability. A law without sanctions is not regarded as law at all. It is regarded as merely voluntary; as an urgent plea. Yet, a very substantial portion of the Halachah is only that. It is directed only to the conscience of individuals. No action by courts was ever contemplated in such matters. Disobedience often entails no punishment by human tribunals. Moreover, the Halachah does not hesitate to prohibit action of which no one other than the actor is aware. It also enjoins the mind with regard to beliefs and attitudes. Halachah is much more than law insofar as it encompasses almost all the behavior and thought of those who live by it.

The very nature of the Halachah as a legal system makes for a great diversity of opinion, as to what rules are binding on Jews committed to it. However, the diversity itself is the result of many diverse approaches to the development of Orthodoxy and the Halachah within the framework of its own methodology and the vast sea that are its sources. This sea is, according to Orthodoxy, the glory of Judaism and the means by which the Jewish people forever remain afloat.

CONSERVATIVE JUDAISM

The American development of Conservative Judaism was parallel to the one in Europe. It is one of the religious responses to the situation in which Jews found themselves after the Emancipation. It started as "Historical Judaism". But in general use, this name was replaced in America in the 20th century by the term Conservative Judaism. In the United States it crystallized its institutions and its philosophy, not so much in dissent from Orthodoxy, but in reaction to Reform Judaism. In a certain sense, it stands between Orthodoxy and Reform. It is dedicated to the preservation in America of the knowledge and practice of historical Judaism as ordained in the Law of Moses expounded by the prophets and sages in Israel in Biblical and Talmudic writings. It is also much more dedicated to **the Halachah** which lies at the heart of Judaism than Reform Judaism.

Conservative Judaism was influenced in the early years by men who had received their education within European historical Judaism. But it was **an** essentially autonomous development in America. Those who identified with Conservative Judaism affirmed the end of the ghettoization of the Jews and their emancipation, and the separation of church and state, as positive goods. They hailed the westernization of Jews in manner, education, and culture. They knew that some changes were inevitable in the ways of Jewish religious life. And they were convinced that these changes could be made in the light of biblical and rabbinic precedent, for they viewed the entire history of Judaism as such a succession of changes.

Conservative Judaism laid the emphasis on the Jewish people throughout history as an organism which refreshed its living spirit by responding creatively to new challenges. The founders of this movement faced the contemporary age in the belief that the traditional forms and precepts of Judaism were valid and that changes in practice were to be made only with great reluctance. They maintained considerable tolerance for those among the Conservatives who were boldly innovative, provided that these innovations did not touch essential commitments of the Conservatives, such as their devotion to the Hebrew language in the liturgy, the observance of the Dietary Laws, and the Sabbath.

Conservative Judaism had its origins in a movement of the 19th century, commonly called as "Science of Judaism". It was based on three fundamental principles. It viewed Judaism as the product of a long, continuous inner development, responsive to its changing historical setting. It was based on the conviction that Judaism owes its survival to the organic continuity that characterized it in all its successive phases. It held the view that history puts a stamp of sanctity on common religious practices that have been observed by the Jewish people over a long period of time.

The first to draw the practical implications of these studies for contemporary Judaism was Zacharias Frankel from Germany, who, as a result, is commonly regarded as the Founding Father of Conservative Judaism. Frankel's sharp reaction to the pronounced anti-halachic views of the early proponents of Reform Judaism must be seen as an additional factor in the genesis of Conservative Judaism's attitude towards the Halachah.

In Conservative Judaism, the law is the permanent requisite for attaining a fuller and deeper level of Jewish religious living and for achieving nobler human sensibilities. The law cannot be abrogated but only amended by the traditional method of interpretation and enactment. Yet, Judaism consists not alone of law but of basic principles. "Thou shalt love thy neighbor as thyself" (Leviticus, 19:18) is a "Great Principle" (K'LAL GADOL). When a conflict arises between the law and such basic principles, the law must give way to the principle of the religious and ethical values of Judaism. In interpreting the law, consideration must be given not only to its letter but to its general aim and spirit.

The central institution of Conservative Judaism in the United States is the Jewish Theological Seminary in America. It was founded to provide an English-speaking westernized clergy to replace the foreign immigrant rabbis. By 1901, an alumni association of the Seminary existed. This body was named the Rabbinical Assembly of America, later called: The Rabbinical Assembly, the International Association of Conservative Rabbis. To its members belong rabbis on all the continents sharing the Conservative outlook.

One of the teachers at the Jewish Theological Seminary in New York was Mordechai Menachem Kaplan. In 1918 he founded the Jewish Center in New York, the first American synagogue center. In it he attempted to integrate religion, education for young and adults, and recreational endeavor. It was, however, Kaplan's philosophy of Judaism which was even more important in changing the shape of Conservative Judaism. In his view, Judaism was a religious civilization, the evolving creation of the Jewish community which expressed its ethos through the pattern of behavior and folkways which it devised. If the inherited ideas and rituals of Judaism were expressions of such past plans, the present generation, while respectful toward that past, was both free and obligated to make its' own changes in the light of its own needs. According to Kaplan, Jewish religion embraces both the purpose and the unconscious product of the Jewish people's search for a meaningful existence for itself. Judaism should be considered from a pragmatic, historical point of view. The focus of the content of Jewish life is the Jewish people, its needs, and its responses to challenge, rather than revealed texts or metaphysical constructions. Tradition can guide but must not dictate. This view came to be know as Reconstructionism, the only Jewish movement which sprang up in America. Kaplan influenced generations of Conservative and Reform rabbis and this influence extended even to secularist circles. But the majority of those who followed him, in whole or in part, were within the Conservative movement. The Reconstructionist group within Conservative Judaism moved increasingly toward defining itself as a group in its own right. It even established a rabbinical school of its own, the Reconstructionist Rabbinical College, in Philadelphia, in 1968.

In the first half of the 20th century, the Jewish Theological Seminary of America succeeded in becoming an academic institution of international eminence. Its library grew to be the single most important collection of books on Judaism that was ever assembled outside of Israel. After World War II Conservative Judaism rose rapidly. It became the religious movement which spoke to the American-born children of East European immigrants, reconciling both their attachments to the traditional emotions of the youth of most of them and their accepting the American culture, and educating their children in congregational schools and in recent years also in hundreds of day schools.

Standing between Orthodoxy and Reform Judaism, Conservative Judaism has shown,and must also in future show,great capacity and strength.

REFORM JUDAISM

Reform Judaism is the first of the modern interpretations of Judaism to emerge in response to the changed political and cultural conditions brought about by the Emancipation. It is also known as Liberal or Progressive Judaism. Reform Judaism's manifestations vary from place to place. They have undergone constant changes in the course of time. They all share the assertion of the legitimacy of change in Judaism and the denial of eternal validity to any given formulation of Jewish belief or codification of Jewish law.

The term "Reform" is not an American usage but a borrowing from German. It flourished in America and lost any widespread significance in its homeland. There the word "Reform", which in the early nineteenth century had functioned as a general term, describing in large measure a tendency or movement, and only to a very limited degree concrete institutions, finally became the designation of the small "left" wing of that tendency and its institutions. Most participants in the movement were designated Liberal. In the 1920's, the term "Progressive" emerged as an international institutional designation covering all of the groupings, without suggesting either theoretical or practical uniformity.

There is little unanimity among Reform Jews whether in matters of belief or in practical observance. Conservative and radical positions co-exist and enjoy mutual respect.

The first reformers in Germany were laymen, working without rabbinic leadership. Their primary concerns were the large-scale defections from Judaism in the age of Emancipation and the absence of Western standards of the decorum in the traditional manner of Jewish worship. They set about reforming the service by abbreviating the liturgy; introducing the sermon in the language of the country; choral singing with musical (organ) accompaniment; supplementing the standard Hebrew prayers with prayers in German. They had no intention of breaking with tradition. On the contrary, they made every effort to demonstrate, by an appeal to the Talmud and the codes, that their reforms were compatable with traditional Jewish law. But their invocation of rabbinic, traditional sources failed to convince the traditionalists. The reformers no longer shared the traditional longing for a return to Zion. Changes in the wording of the liturgy were made to reflect this new attitude.

A new generation of rabbis with a university education in addition to the traditional training then showed themselves sympathetic to the cause of Reform Judaism. Rabbinical conferences in 1844, 1845 and 1846 tried to provide justifications from traditional sources for liturgical reforms, particularly connected with the use of the non-Hebrew language in worship and with organ accompaniment of the service. They also sought to lighten some of the traditional severity of Sabbath observance and laws of marriage and divorce. Although their attitude toward the Talmud, the codes, the Halachah was often ambivalent, the German Reform Rabbis continued to justify their reforms with references to rabbinic sources. They differed, thus, significantly from other contemporary, more radical, manifestitations of Reform Judaism. In America, too, Reform Judaism passed through a stage in which the Bible was accepted and the Talmud rejected. The reason for these stages and manifestations was that in America, Reform mostly took place outside, whereas in Germany, the Reform was "from within", manifesting itself within old-established communities. In contrast to American Reform Judaism, German Reform Judaism always retained a pronounced tradionalist aspect, calling itself "Liberal" rather than "Reform". In Germany, the latter term was restricted to the extremist Berlin Reformgemeinde, the only congregation in Germany with an all-German service, bareheaded worship and the Sunday Sabbath.

It was Abraham **Geiger** who laid the basis for the Liberal movement. According to him, Judaism is a constantly evolving organism. Biblical Judaism was not identical with classical talmudic Judaism. The modern age calls for further evolution in accordance with the changed circumstances. The role played by tradition enabled Judaism to adapt itself constantly. For Geiger, tradition and change were synonymous. The modern rabbis are entitled to adapt medieval Judaism, as the early rabbis had the right to adapt biblical Judaism. He valued tradition highly, and saw in it the inherent justification of Reform. For him change in Judaism had always been organic, never revolutionary. The modern changes must, therefore, develop out of the past, and not represent a revolutionary break with it. Since Judaism as a whole is involved in the process of change, Reform Judaism is a strong pillar of Judaism. Monotheism and the moral law are the constant elements of Judaism. Ceremonies have the function of expressing those ideas. Yet, they are of value only as long as they fulfill that function. They are, therefore, Judaism's changing element. So is the Jewish people. Though once a nation, it was one no longer. The messianic hope is to be interpreted in universal terms rather than in terms of national restoration.

Geiger's theory became basic to all future formulations of Reform doctrine, particularly of that aspect known as "Progressive Revelation". In the light of that doctrine, Reform Judaism was later able to affirm God's participation in the formation of the Talmud.

In Europe acceptance to Reform's radicalism - created by Samuel Holdheim - was confined to the Berlin Reformgemeinde which Holdheim served as a rabbi. But in America, the radical idea fell on more fertile soil. Here, too, there was a division between moderate and radical Reform. The former championed by Rabbi Isaac Mayer Wise (1819-1900) and the latter by David Einhorn (1809-1879). By 1855 the radical position had become dominant in American Reform Judaism. It was expressed in the "Pittsburgh Platform".

Wise was aware of the existential presence of the halachic structure on the American scene. Hence, his willingness to acknowledge that the Talmud would be the basis upon which any discussion of Reform would take place. He was ready to do so because of his unyielding belief in the power of the American environment to reform constructively the inherited structures of Jewish life. For him, the changes would emerge organically out of the past. The clogged channels of Jewish creativity would be cleared. What would flow forth would be at once new and at the same time a rejuvenation of the past. Eventually, it was Isaac Mayer Wise - and not the radical David Einhorn - who founded and built the institutions that never fell away from Wise's recognition of the importance of the religious legal system. However, it was to be transformed in the future.

Yet, Wise's insistence on the Moasic authorship of the Pentateuch did not extend to the Talmudic-rabbinic tradition. The attitudes and positions of the German Wissenschaft des Judentums (Science of Judaism) were accepted. The historically conditioned nature of the Law, the Halachah, was taken for granted. As Geiger had recognized, relativizing did not necessarily result in rejection. It supported the demands for modifications of the religious legal system based whenever, and as far as possible, on some foothold within the system itself.

It was this tendency that was eventually widely adhered to in the American Reform Rabbinate. When the optimism and the utopian euphoria of the 19th century was upset by historical reality, the American reformers realized that the role of traditional observance in Jewish survival had been considerably underestimated in the "Pittsburgh Platform". In 1937, the "Columbus Platform" emerged. It retained the stress on Judaism's compatability with science, the centrality of the moral law, the progressive nature of revelation but it also emphasized other points. The Torah, both written and oral, enshrines Israel's evergrowing consciousness of God and of the moral law. The obligation of all Jewry to aid in the upbuilding of a Jewish homeland in the land of the Bible was affirmed. Judaism as a way of life requires the preservation of the Sabbath, the Festivals, and the Holy Days, the retention and development of such customs, symbols, and ceremonies as possess inspirational value, the cultivation of distinctive forms of religious art and music and the use of Hebrew together with the language of the country of worship and instruction.

Since the adoption of the "Columbus Platform", there has been a greater openness on the part of American Reform Judaism to many traditional observances. The study of Hebrew has returned to the curriculum of the schools. Anti-Zionism, at one time considered in Reform Judaism a mandate of "universalism", had given way to large-scale support of the State of Israel. But this in itself is not yet evidence of a deeper theological rethinking. It has not yet had a marked bearing on real Reform Jewish practice. A school of thought, influenced by Martin Buber and Franz Rosenzweig and by representatives of other trends in religious existentialism, as well as by considerations of Kelal Ysrael (The Unity of Israel) is mainly confined to the younger theologians of the movement. They are engaged in the "rediscovery" of traditional theological concepts such as covenant, revelation, and law.

The world's Reform congregations are united in the World Union For Progressive Judaism, founded in 1926. Three rabbinical seminaries, in London, Paris, and the Hebrew Union College - Jewish Institute of Religion (with the main campus in Cincinnati, Ohio) train the rabbis for the movement. The oldest, the Berlin Hochschule Fuer die Wissenschaft des Judentums, founded in 1872, was a victim of the Holocaust. The strongest constituent of Reform Judaism in the world is the American branch. Because of its numerical and financial strength, it assumed the world leadership of the movement. Outside the U.S. Reform Judaism tends to be far more traditionally observant than it is in America.

The most recent discussions of the religious system within American Reform Judaism have tended to avoid the term Halachah. The reason for this is obvious. Halachah seems to be the ground on which Orthodoxy has taken its stand. It has been preempted. Any attempt to repossess it will either lead to confusion - to talk about Halachah is to surrender to the "enemy" - or will be futile. In place of Halachah the more potent and more dangerous word MITZVAH had been used. The word is more dangerous, because, Mitzvah (Commandment) requires one who commands, a commander. This would quite easily suggest that the religious legal system of Judaism is the word, the commandment of God and, thus, we are once again in the divinely ordained, historically unconditioned system. This, however, is not what is intended. There is no consensus today within Reform Judaism in this matter. But the discussion suggests the seriousness with which it is being argued in some quarters within the American Reform movement.

Pulled simultaneously in opposite directions, Reform Judaism thus faces the problem which has remained without solution since the movement's beginning: the question of religious authority and the resulting difficulty of setting limits to a liberal religion.

CHABAD -- THE LUBAVITCH CHASSIDIM

Among the various brands of Chassidim now in existance the Lubavitch group is by far the most active and visible one in Jewish centers around the world. Its adherents are widely known as members of the Chabad movement. This name is the abbreviated sum of three Hebrew words: Chochmah - wisdom; Binah - understanding; Daat - knowledge. It is the special system within Chassidim, founded by Rabbi Shneur Zalman of Lyady (1745-1812), which stresses the intellect in the study of the Torah, emphasizing its constant study coupled with unceasing spiritual exercise, as indispensable for achieving lasting results. It embraces the contemplation on the "Secrets of the Torah" (The Kabbalah) more than other Chassidic systems.

The practical Jewish ideal, according to the teachings of the founder of the system, is that of the Beinoni--the average man. He is required to resist evil throughout his life, to reject it through his inner decision. To achieve this aim, man is required to utilize his spiritual powers. The struggle against evil must be sustained and it is helped by the use of meditation. Meditation on the greatness of the Creator, on love and reverence for Him, leads to an elevation of the soul to a higher degree. Strict attention is required also to be paid to the accepted Jewish behavior--such as observance of the commandments, Torah study and the worship of God in joyousness while repressing melancholy. Studying of the mystic system, the Kabbalah, is a means of strengthening faith in God. The love of God and reverence for Him are only a step of arousing the soul toward the true attachment--through Torah study and complying with the rules.

Shneur Zalman was called the "Old Rebbe". The present Lubavitcher Rabbi is Menachem Mendel Schneerson (b. 1902). In the Lubavitch system, great significance is attached to the personality and "soul root" of each leader or Rebbe, past as well as present. He enjoys authority of an absolute kind among his followers. His command is accepted with unquestioning obedience.

The founder of the movement Shneur Zalman, did not intend to present a complete theology. He wanted to be a guide to the path leading to the true service of God. He constructed a psychological system based on Kabbalistic principles, penetrating to the depths of the human soul. He developed the idea, later followed through by other Chabad thinkers, that deep in the inner place of every Jewish soul there is a divine spark. This concept acquired great social significance in Lubavitch, which has become

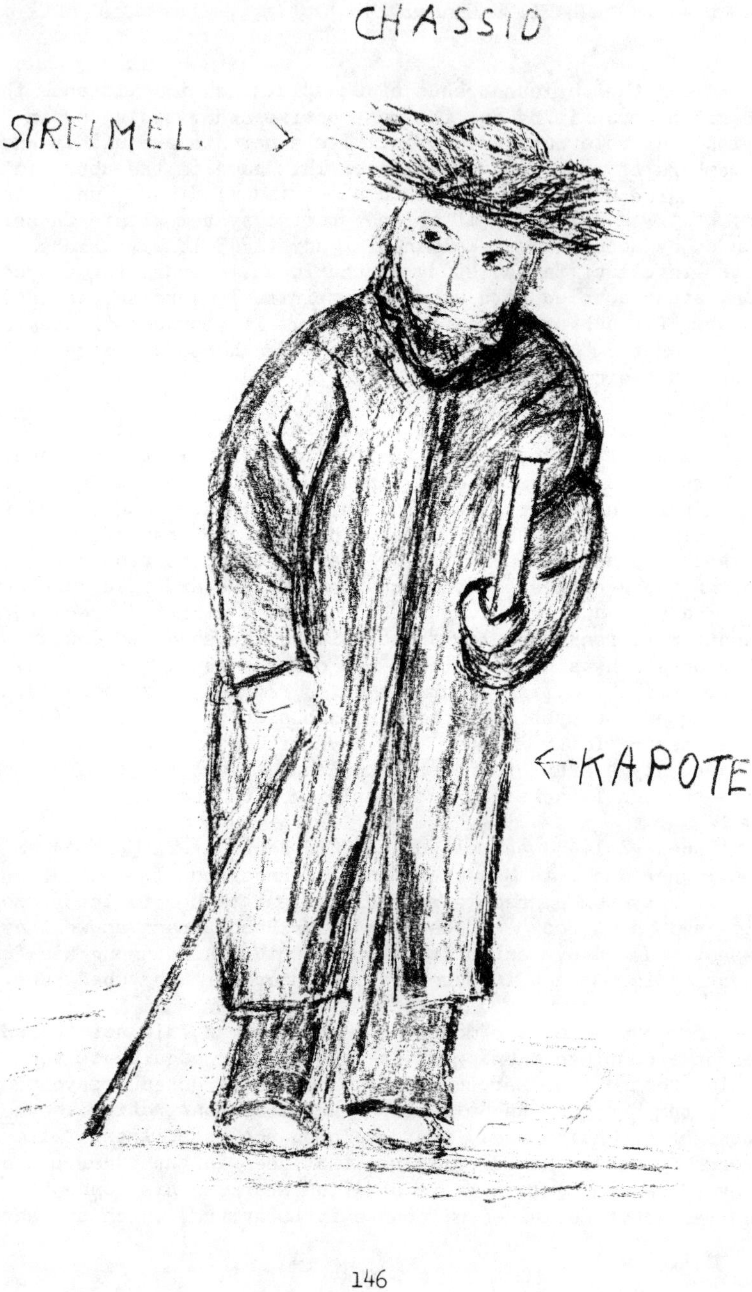
CHASSID
STREIMEL
KAPOTE

a missionary movement to the Jews--and, to some extent, even to
gentile converts, in the belief that the gentile, too, acquires
his "divine soul" on his acceptance of Judaism. No Jew is held
to be beyond redemption, no matter how far he has strayed from
the religion and observance of the commandments. This movement
has attained surprising successes in this field, winning over
many uncommitted Jews to a full participation in a life of Torah
and Mitzvot. It is not a Jewish Salvation Army. But it is
marked by an "evangelical" eagerness wedded to an emotionalism
that is somewhat astonishing in view of the founder's strong intellectual approach.

The primary work of the Chabad system and its important
contribution to Jewish philosophy is the book of the founder,
"Likutei Amarim" (Collected Sayings). The book starts with the
letters "Tanya" (It has been taught) and has continued to be
widely known by this name ever since. It met with instant
acclaim. The Tanya is divided into five sections. The Chabad
Chassidim refer to it as the written law of Chabad and designate
it for daily study.

The Lubavitch movement is numerically the strongest of all
the Chassidic groups. They are active in all parts of the United
States (with the headquarters in Brooklyn, New York) and in communities all over the world. At their headquarters regular
gatherings (called "Farbrengen") are held at which the Rebbe
speaks in Yiddish for hours on end. These talks are later translated into other languages.

The Lubavitch Chassidim have build a strong educational network. A spate of education material pours from the presses of
their printing house. Their schools flourish in many parts of
the world. The self-sacrificing spirit of the Lubavitch educators has won the admiration even of those Jews hostile to Chassidism. In Soviet Russia, they willingly risked their lives in
order to hand down the tradition to the next generation. Lubavitch "missions" have been established in universities. The
Rebbe, the leader of the movement today, Menachem Mendel Schneerson, was educated at the Sorbonne in Paris, France. He has
often stated that this has made him aware of the special problems
in matters of faith the university student has to face.

Those continuing the system created by the founder Schneur
Zalman of Lyady merely explain and expand what he laid down.
The principal contribution of his own descendants to the Chabad
teachings was their selection of various subjects out of the
total of those treated by him. Shneur Zalman's work was given
direction and definition principally by his son and successor
Dov Baer (1773-1827). He settled in the little town of Lubavitch,
which became the center of the Chabad movement. He placed even

greater emphasis on the principle of meditation and expanded it. He also strengthened the intellectual aspect of Chabad, designating the study of Chassidism not only as a means to an end but also an end in itself.

The Chabad movement is greatly concerned with the carrying out of the practical commandments of Judaism. Wherever Jews meet in large numbers, Lubavitch Chassidim are found urging them to put on Tefillin, to perform the commandment of taking the Lulav and Etrog on Sukkot. Packages of Matzah are dispatched to thousands of homes of poor Jews before Passover, together with the Rebbe's seasonal greetings.

In their missionary thrust, Chabad Chassidim have adopted the slogan "Ufaratzta" (And thou shalt spread abroad). It is based on the promise to Jacob: "And thy seed shall be as the dust of the earth, and thou shalt spread abroad to the west, and to the east, and to the north, and to the south. And in thee and in thy seed shall all the families of the earth be blessed" (Genesis 28:14). Aware of the similarities between its approach and Christian missionary activities, Chabad is highly sensitive to the charge of imitation. They vehemently deny that the term "Jewish missionaries" fits the movement. Lubavitch maintains that the correct translation of the Hebrew word "Teshuvah" is not "Repentance" but "Return" to God and His Torah. A Jew, according to that, is inherently good and wishes to do good. It is only because of various reasons for which he is not always totally responsible that he committed a sin. Thus it is that Chabad Chassidism sees every Jew, no matter how estranged, as potentially observant and, indeed, as a potential member of the movement. Every person has to be given every encouragement to allow the divine spark within him to awaken itself. Of all the Chassidic groups Lubavitch is the most tolerant. Nevertheless, it is far removed from tolerance towards unorthodox or untraditional views or conduct. Its philosophy refuses to recognize that there can be any truth in viewpoints other than its own. It says that deep down every Jew really knows that the Chassidic way of life is completely true and the only way to cope with the human situation.

True to this thought, the movement stresses education of old and young as the sure remedy for the sinful way. When the truth is known, the Jew is bound to respond to it. All heresy and all laxity in the observances of Judaism are the fruit of ignorance. The Chabad Chassidim strongly believe in the spiritual value of song and of dance. The founder said that the tongue is the pen of the heart but that the melody is the pen of the soul. When the Chassid sings, he raises himself above the material universe to achieve "Devekut"--cleaving to God. The majority of the Lubavitch melodies are without words. Dancing is said to be significant because it is the highest manifestation of inner happiness. The feet moving in the dance are likened in Chabad thought to the non-intellectual qualities of the soul. Dancing to the glory of God is, thus, an expression of the simple, basic faith of the Jew. However, unlike many other Chassidim, Lubavitch Chassidim generally engage in dance only on important occasions in the Jewish year. As a holy exercise the religious dance must not be made dull through familiarity.

Segregation of the sexes in Chassidic life and the synagogue is upheld, according to the orthodox traditional manner. Women have their role in the movement and the education of girls is given special attention. The lifestyle of the Chabad Chassidim sometimes differs in some respects from the patterns observed in other branches of Chassidim. In matters of dress they neither wear the Bekeshe or Kapote, a garment generally made of very expensive cloth, such as velvet or glossy silk, nor "Streimel" (fur-brimmed hat) and white socks, nor do they cultivate "corkscrew" Peot, sidelocks,grown in accordance with the prohibition of the Bible that "Ye shall not round the corners of your heads" (Leviticus, 19:27). Their melodies have a strong "Russian" association (from where they originate) and the Lubavitch type of beard is long and bushy (resembling the old-fashioned Russian beard). Next to prayer, Torah study is the supreme command. The study of Talmud and Codes is also desired. From the days of its founding fathers, Chabad has held to the view that the old ban on public teaching of the Kabbalah has been rescinded and that, in this period in history, when the footsteps of the Messiah will soon be heard, only a constant familiarity with the words of the living God can succeed in awakening the powers of the divine soul.

Chabad has a very positive attitude towards the State of Israel,in contrast to the virulent anti-Zionism of other Chassidic groups. Nevertheless, the leader has not been to Israel and has been sharply critical of some aspects of life in the Jewish state.

The attitude toward modern science is also generally positive. The Chabad movement in the United States operates community supported rehabilitation centers for drug addicts for Jews and non-Jews with very good results.

Chassidism with its concern for the poor and underprivileged as well as the hallowing of the everyday, brought new hope to many in the darkest days of Jewish history. It dramatizes Jewish teachings and the Jewish way of life. It brushed away the cobwebs and revitalized Judaism not by introducing revolutionary doctrines, but simply by leading the people back to the principles preached by the great prophets and teachers of Israel. They also had and have a great influence on Jewish writers. The inspiration of Chassidim can be detected in the poetry, the stories, and the novels of such Nobel Prize winners as Nelly Sachs, Shmuel Joseph Agnon and Isaac Bashevis Singer, and the writings of Isaac Leib Peretz, Shalom Asch, Franz Kafka, Martin Buber,

Abraham Joshua Heschel and Elie Wiesel. Their soaring ecstasy and their radiance brought a new message to a super-sophisticated and over-organized Jewish society.

BIBLIOGRAPHY

THE HOLY SCRIPTURES

Genesis	Hosea
Exodus	Amos
Leviticus	Obadjah
Numbers	Jonah
Deuteronomy	Micah
	Zephaniah
	Zechariah
Joshua	
Judges	
I Samuel	Psalms
II Samuel	Proverbs
I Kings	Job
II Kings	Song of Songs
	Lamentations
	Ecclesiastes
Isaiah	Esther
Jeremiah	Daniel
Ezekiel	Ezra
	Nehemiah
	Chronicles

TALMUD AND MIDRASH

    Mishna Bikkurim
    Mishna Kelim
    Mishna Rosh Hashana
    Mishna Sukka

    Sayings of the Fathers

    Bab. Talmud Aboda Sara
    Bab. Talmud Baba Batra
    Bab. Talmud Baba Kamma
    Bab. Talmud Baba Metzia
    Bab. Talmud Berachot
    Bab. Talmud Chullin
    Bab. Talmud Eruvin
    Bab. Talmud Gittin
    Bab. Talmud Jebamot
    Bab. Talmud Ketubot
    Bab. Talmud Kiddushin
    Bab. Talmud Maccot
    Bab. Talmud Megilla
    Bab. Talmud Pessachim
    Bab. Talmud Rosh Hashana
    Bab. Talmud Sanhedrin
    Bab. Talmud Shabbat
    Bab. Talmud Sota
    Bab. Talmud Sukka
    Bab. Talmud Taanit
    Bab. Talmud Yoma

    Jer. Talmud Chagiga
    Jer. Talmud Pea
    Jer. Talmud Pessachim
    Jer. Talmud Rosh Hashana
    Jer. Talmud Shekalim
    Jer. Talmud Taanit

MIDRASHIM

    Midrash Bereshit Rabba
    Midrash Shemot Rabba
    Midrash Vajikra Rabba
    Midrash Bamibdar Rabba
    Midrash Devarim Rabba
    Midrash Tanchuma Bereshit
    Midrash Tanchuma Noa
    Midrash Tanchuma Shemini
    Midrash Tanchuma Teruma
    Midrash Tanchuma Tasria
    Midrash Tanchuma Pesikta Rabbati
    Midrash to Psalms
    Midrash to Proverbs
    Midrash Lekach Tov to Genesis
    Midrash Abot de Rabbi Natan
    Midrash Tanna De Be Eliahu
    Midrash Leolam
    Midrash Yalkut Shimoni
    Midrash Pirkei Rabbi Eliezer
    Midrash Pirkei De Rav Kahane

OTHER

    Encyclopaedia Judaica.

    The Holy Scriptures - According to the Masoretic Text. Jewish Publication Society, Philadelphia, PA.

    The Prophets - Neviim. Jewish Publication Society, Philadelphia, PA.

    Siddur - Daily Prayerbook.

    Machzor - Prayerbook for Holidays.

INDEX

of Persons, Places and Terms

A

Abbajeh, 9, 47
Abraham, 49, 63, 105, 109
Achad Haam, 7
Adam, 131
Adar, 3, 4, 37, 39
Adar Bet, 3, 37
Addition, 43, 123, 124
Additional Prayer, 11, 13, 31, 43
Affikoman, 21
Afternoon Prayer, 43
Aggadah, 121, 124
Agnon, Shmuel Joseph, 149
Akiba, Rabbi, 25, 50, 77, 107
Albertus Magnus, 129
Alexander of Hales, 129
All the Vows, 16
Amalek, 37
Amidah, 43
Ammud, 41
Amos, 13, 105, 107, 119
Angels, 85
Annual Anniversary of Death, 62
Anointed, 75
Anthropomorphism, 81
Antiochus Epiphanes, 33
Apocrypha, 33, 120, 131
Arabic, 113, 127
Aramaic, 61, 113, 115, 117, 123
Aramaic Translation of the Bible, 117
Aristotelianism, 129
Ark, Holy, 31, 41, 110
Asceticism, 101
Asch, Shalom, 149
Asseret Yemey Teshuva, 11
Atonement, 15, 16, 89
Av, 3, 39
Avicebron, 128
Avot de Rabbi Natan, 123

B

Baal, 109
Babylonia, 3, 39, 43, 63, 105, 118, 119, 120, 121, 123
Bachya Ben Joseph Ibn Paquda, 128
Baghdad, 127
Bamidbar, 118
Bar Kochba, 39, 77
Bar Mitzvah, 51
Bat Mitzvah, 51
Beginning of Time, 1
Beinoni, 145
Bekeshe, 149
Beliefs and Opinions, 127
Bereshit, 117, 121
Berlin Reformgemeinde, 142, 143
Bet Haknesset, 41
Bet Hatefillah, 41
Betar, Fortress of, 39
Bible, 3, 22, 45, 67, 71, 85, 93, 113, 115, 117, 120, 121, 122, 124, 127, 128, 142, 143
Binah, 145
Bitter Herbs, 21
Blessing, 5, 7, 47, 49, 51, 53, 55, 122, 132
Book of Books, 117
Books, Judaism's, 115
Boxes of Leather, 47
Bread of Affliction, 19
Brit Milah, 49
Brooklyn, N.Y., 147
Bruch, Max, 16
Buber, Martin, 144, 149

C

Cairo, 37, 124
Calendar, Jewish, 1, 3
Canaanites, 109
Candelabra, 33, 43
Candle Lighting Ceremony, 5, 33
Canopy, 53
Cantor, 11, 16, 31, 41, 43, 49
Caro Joseph, Rabbi, 125
Catholicism, 134
Cello, 16
Cemetery, 61
Chabad, 145, 147, 148, 149
Chag Hamatzot, 19
Chag Hashavuot, 25
Challah, 5
Chanukkah, 33, 35, 37
Chanukkiah, 33, 41
Charosset, 21
Chasan, 43
Chassid, 131
Chassidism, 132, 145, 147, 148, 149
Chatan Bereshit, 31
Chatan Torah, 31
Chaver, 129
Chazon, 39
Chevrah Kadishah, 61
Chochmah, 145
Choir, 43, 141
Chosen People, The, 105, 109
Chovot Ha-Levavot, 128
Christianity, 67, 71, 117, 127, 128, 129, 130, 148
Christmas Season, 33
Chronicles, Books of, 120
Chumash, 117
Chuppah, 53
Churches, 113, 117, 137
Cincinnati, 144
Circumcision, 49
Civil and Criminal Law, 122
Cleaving to God, 148
Clement of Alexandria, 127
Code of Jewish Law, 125, 149
Collected Sayings, 147

Columbus Platform, 143
Comfort, Sabbath, 39
Commandment, 15, 29, 51, 57, 61, 63, 71, 72, 81, 93, 97, 101, 105, 109, 115, 118, 121, 125, 128, 144, 145, 147, 148
Community Service, 43, 45, 47
Completion, 123
Composer, German, 16
Concert Repertoire, 16
Concluding Festival, 31
Conclusion, 45
Confirmation, 27, 51
Conservatives, 3, 25, 27, 43, 134, 137, 139
Converts, 16, 105, 147
Cordova, 124
Counting of Time, 25
Covenant, 49, 75, 89, 105, 109, 133, 144
Creation, 5, 13, 67, 68, 71, 75, 81, 117, 127, 130
Credo of Judaic Faith, 43
Crown of the Jewish Year, 15, 89

D

Daat, 145
Daily Sacrifice, 43
Damages, Order of, 122
Dance, Religious, 148, 149
Daniel, 102, 120
Daughter of the Commandment, 51
David, King, 33, 75, 105, 109, 118, 119, 120
Day, Jewish, 1
Day, The, 15
Day of Atonement, 3, 11, 15, 29, 31, 39, 40, 45, 55, 79, 89
Day of the Blowing of the Horn, 11
Day of Reckoning, 11, 13
Day of Remembrance, 11, 13

Day of Thanksgiving, 31
Days of Awe, 11
Days of Penitence, 11
Dead Sea, 101
Death, 61, 89
Derech Eretz Sutta, 78, 96
Desert, 21, 118
Dessert, Official, 21
Deuteronomy, 28, 31, 43, 45, 57, 59, 63, 64, 86, 94, 98, 105, 110, 111, 114, 118
Devarim, 118
Devekut, 148
Diaspora, 31, 75, 76, 109, 131
Dietary Laws, 57, 137
Dipping of Green, 21
Divorce, 55, 142
Divre Hayamim, 120
Dogmas, 63
Dov Baer, 147
Dreidel, 33
Drug Addicts, 149
Duns Scotus, 129
Duties of the Heart, 128

E

Eastern European Jewry, 41, 132, 139
Ecclesiastes, 62, 120, 121, 127
Ecclesiasticus, 120
Echa, 120
Egypt, 5, 19, 37, 49, 63, 71, 105, 109, 117, 118, 124
Eighteen Prayers, 43, 78
Einhorn, David, 143
Eliah, The Prophet, 22, 49, 75, 77, 119
Elishah, the Prophet, 119
Elchanan, Rabbi Isaac, 134
Elul, 3, 11
Emunot Vedeot, 127
English, 75, 113
Enoch, Book of, 131
Esotericism, 130
Esther, Book of, 37, 38, 120, 121
Eternal Light, 41
Eternity, 1, 5, 67, 127

Ethics, 11, 15, 67, 71, 81, 85, 93, 101, 109, 118, 121, 123, 131, 138
Etrog, 29, 31, 148
Europe, 124, 132, 137, 143
Evangeligal, 147
Eve, Kol Nidre, 16
Evening Prayer, 43, 45
Evil, 85
Evil Inclination, 85, 89
Exodus, Book of, 7, 22, 23, 27, 57, 72, 74, 81, 83, 106, 108, 112, 118
Ezekiel, 90, 111, 119
Ezra, Book of, 120

F

Family, 5, 57, 97, 101, 105
Farbrengen, 147
Fast Days, 39, 45, 122
Fast, Total, 15
Ferdinand, King, 39
Festival of the Booth, 3, 29
Festival of the First Fruit Harvest, 25
Festival of the Lights, 33
Festival of the Rededication of the Temple, 33
Festival of the Tabernacles, 3, 19, 29, 31, 120
Festival of the Ten Commandments, 25
Festival of the Unleavened Bread, 3, 19
Festival of the Weeks, 19, 25, 120
Festivals, Order of, 122
Fettmilch, 37
Fit to Consume, 57
Flowers, 25, 61
Food Consumption, 57
Four Questions, 21
Frankel, Zacharias, 138
Frankfurt, Germany, 37
Free Choice, 85, 89
Freedom Festival, 19
French, 124

Friday Afternoon, 5
Fringes, 45
Frontlets, 45

G

Garden of Eden, 53, 89
Gedalia, Jewish Governor, 39
Geiger, Abraham, 142, 143
Gemarah, 123
Genesis, 7, 31, 50, 55, 62, 68,
  74, 86, 88, 97, 106, 110,
  114, 117, 121, 148
Genocide, 75, 85
German, 16, 113, 124, 138, 141,
  142
Gett, 55
Gifts, 37
God, 1, 5, 7, 11, 13, 25, 29, 43,
  47, 49, 53, 55, 57, 61, 63,
  67, 71, 75, 76, 81, 85, 89,
  93, 101, 105, 109, 113, 120,
  127, 128, 129, 130, 132, 142,
  143, 145, 148, 149
God's Kingdom, 13
God's Remembrance, 13
Goliath, 33
Good Inclination, 86
Grace, 5, 21, 47, 78, 85, 89
Gragger, 37
Graduation Ceremonies, 27
Great Principle, 138
Greek, 33, 41, 75, 117, 120, 123,
  130
Greek Translation of Bible, 117
Greens, 21
Greetings, 13
Gregory of Nysea, 127
Groom of the Beginning, 31
Groom of the Torah, 31
Guide of the Perplexed, 129

H

Habakkuk, Prophet, 119
Ha-Chodesh, 37
Haftarah, 39, 45, 78
Haggadah, 19, 21

Haggai, Prophet, 119
Hagiographa, 119
Halachah, 121, 123, 124, 125,
  131, 133, 137, 138, 143,
  144
Half Holidays, 19, 29
Hallel, 29
Haman, 37, 39
Haman's Ears, 37
Hamantaschen, 37
Hasmoneans, 33
Havdalah, 5, 7
Hear, O Israel, 43, 57, 61,
  63
Hebrew Language, The, 43,
  113, 115, 123, 137, 144
Hebrew Union College - Jewish
  Institute of Religion, 144
Heschel, Abraham Joshua, 150
Hidden Writings, 120
Hieronymus, 117
Hillel II, 1
Hillel Sandwich, 21
Historical Judaism, 137
Hochschule Fuer die Wissen-
  schaft des Judentums,
  Berlin, Germany, 144
Holdheim, Samuel, 143
Holiday, Highest, 15, 16, 89
Holiday of Freedom, 22
Holiday of Thanksgiving, 29
Holocaust, 85, 144
Holy Brotherhood, 61
Holy Land, 109
Holy Language, 113
Holy Things, Order of, 122,
  123
Holying, The, 53, 97
Home, Jewish, 5, 19, 45, 57,
  97, 101
Homolies, 121, 122
Hors D'Oevres, 21
Hoseah, Prophet, 91, 119
Hoshanah, 29
Hoshanah Rabba, 29
House of Assembly, 41
House of God, 11, 41
House of Prayer, 41

Hut, 29

I

I and Thou Relationship, 81
Ibn Gabriol, Solomon, 128
Individual, The, 81, 85, 89,
 93, 97, 101, 135
Intermediary, 81
Isaac, 105
Isabel, Queen, 39
Isaiah, 9, 17, 39, 41, 68, 73,
 75, 76, 77, 86, 91, 106,
 107, 108, 119
Islam, 127, 128
Isserles, Rabbi Moses, 125
Israel, Land of, 3, 19, 25,
 29, 31, 39, 75, 109, 110,
 113, 139, 149
Israel, People of, 7, 13, 33,
 53, 75, 105, 109, 110, 113,
 117, 120, 131
Iyar, 3

J

Jacob, 76, 91, 99, 105, 148
Jahrzeit, 62
Jalkut Shimoni, 91, 103, 122
Jehuda Halevi, 39, 128, 129
Jehuda Ha-Nassi, 102, 122
Jeremiah, 68, 73, 74, 77, 102, 111, 119
Jeremiah's Lamentations, 39, 120, 121
Jerusalem, 3, 9, 19, 21, 37, 39,
 43, 49, 55, 89, 109, 110, 119,
 120, 123
Jew, Traditional, 57
Jewish Center, The, 138
Jewish Theological Seminary, 138, 139
Job, Book of, 85, 86, 99, 120, 127
Jochanan, Rabbi, 9, 23, 24
Joel, Prophet, 119
Jonah, Prophet, 119
Joshua Ben Chananja, Rabbi, 9
Joshua Ben Sira, Book of Wisdom, 120
Joshua, Book of, 23, 117, 118
Joy of Living, 132
Joy of the Torah, 31
Juda Maccabee, 33
Juda, State of, 119
Judges, Book of, 118
Judit, Book of, 120

K

Kabbalah, 130, 131, 132, 145, 149
Kaddish, 47, 61, 62, 79
Kafka, Franz, 149
Kaplan, Mordechai Menachem, 138, 139
Kapote, 149
Kasher, 57
Kashrut, 57
Ketubah, 53
Ketuvim, 117, 119
Khazars, The, 128
Kiddush, 5, 21
Kiddushin, 53
Kings, Book of, 23, 119
Kislev, 3, 33
K'Lal Gadol, 138
K'Lal Israel, 144
Kodashim, 122, 123
Kohelet, 120
Kohen, 49
Kol Nidre, 16, 45
Kuzari, Book of the, 128

L

Lag Be'Omer, 25
Latin Translation of Bible, 117
Leshanah Tovah, 13
Letter of Divorce, 55
Leviticus, 13, 17, 27, 32,
 57, 59, 63, 93, 94, 95,
 98, 102, 110, 118, 138, 149
Liberal Judaism, 141, 142
Likutei Amarim, 147

Liturgy, 13, 15, 131, 137, 141, 142
Locking of the Gate, 16
London, England, 144
Longest Prayer in Jewish Liturgy, 13
Luach, 1
Lubavitch, 145, 147, 148, 149
Lulav, 29, 31, 148
Lyady, 145, 147

M

Maariv, 43
Maccabees, 33
Maccabean Books, 33, 120
Machzor, 45
Magen David, 41
Maimonides, Moses, 63, 124, 125, 129, 130
Malachi, Prophet, 119
Malchuyot, 13
Maoz Tzur, 33
Marcheshvan, 3
Marranos, 16
Marriage, 49, 53, 55, 57, 97, 122, 142
Marriage Document, 53
Mashiach, 75
Matzah, 19, 21, 148
May His Memory Be Blessed, 62
Measure, 121
Measure of Wheat, 25
Mechiltah, 121
Meditation, 145, 147
Megillah, 37
Meister Eckhart, 129
Mekor Chayim, 128
Melachim, 119
Memorial for the Dead, 47
Mendelssohn, Moses, 129
Menorah, 33, 43
Meron, 25
Messiah, 75, 76, 77, 89, 105, 127, 149
Messianic Age, 75, 89, 142
Mezuzah, 57
Micah, Prophet, 64, 94, 119

Middle Age Laments, 39
Midrash, 121, 122
Midrash, Abot de Rabbi Natan, 112
Midrash, Bamidbar Rabba, 107, 112
Midrash, Bereshit Rabba, 9, 56, 69, 78, 83, 88, 102, 107, 122
Midrash, Devarim Rabba, 24
Midrash, Lekach Tov, 100
Midrash, Leolam, 96, 100
Midrash, Proverbs, 38
Midrash, Psalms, 74, 90
Midrash, Shemot Rabba, 24, 65, 74, 83, 91
Midrash Tanchuma - Bereshit, 88
Midrash Tanchuma - Noah, 114
Midrash Tanchuma - Pesikta Rabba, 74
Midrash Tanchuma - Shemini, 59
Midrash Tanchuma - Tasria, 50
Midrash Tanchuma - Teruma, 69
Midrash Vayikra Rabba, 74, 112
Minchah Prayer, 43
Minyan, 47, 51
Minor Holidays, 33
Mishle, 119
Mishloach Manot, 37
Mishnah, Bikkurim, 28
Mishnah, Kelim, 111
Mishnah, Rosh Hashanah, 13, 32
Mishnah, Sukka, 32
Mishna, 19, 122, 123
Mishne Torah, 124
Mission, 147, 148
Mitzvah, 144, 147
Moabite, 105, 120
Moed, 122
Mohel, 49
Monday, 45
Month of Mourning, 61
Months, Jewish, 3
Monotheism, 63, 67, 71, 105, 119, 142

Moon Cycle, 3
Moon Year, 3
Mordechai, 37
Moreh Nevuchim, 129
Morning Prayer, 11, 43
Mortar, 21
Moses, 53, 71, 81, 102, 118, 127, 133, 137
Moses, Five Books of, 41, 45, 117, 118, 121, 122
Mosques, 113
Mourning, 25, 61
Murr, 6
Mussaf Prayer, 11, 13, 31, 43
Mutazilites, The, 127
Myrtle Branches, 29
Mysticism, Jewish, 29, 75, 127, 130, 131, 132

N

Nachum, Prophet, 119
Nachamu, 39
Nashim, 122
Nazis, 85
Nebukadnessar, King, 39
Nehemia, 120
Neila Service, 16
Ner Tamid, 41
Neviim, 117, 118
New Christians, 16
New Month, 3, 45
New Testament, 117
New Year, 3, 11, 13, 29
New Year's Service, 11, 13, 79
Nezikin, 122
Ninth of Av, 39, 120
Nissan, 3, 19
Noah, 13
Numbers, 43, 45, 50, 72, 89, 118
Nuptial Ceremony, 53, 55

O

Obadja, Prophet, 119
Old Testament, 68, 71, 117
Omer, 25

Onkelos, 117
Oral Law, 121, 122, 125, 128, 133
Orchestra, 16
Order, 19, 21, 122
Organ, 43, 141, 142
Origen, 127
Original Sin, 85, 86
Orthodox, 3, 25, 41, 43, 55, 133, 134, 135, 137, 144, 149
Ozney Haman, 37

P

Palestine, 33, 63, 123, 125
Palm Branch, 29
Para, 37
Paris, 144, 147
Parochet, 41
Paschal Lamb, 21
Passover, 3, 19, 21, 22, 25, 37, 109, 120, 123, 148
Patriarchs, 13
Pentateuch, 31, 57, 122, 127, 143
Peot, 149
Peretz, Isaac Leib, 149
Persian Jews, 37
Personal God, 67, 81
Personification of God, 67, 81
Peshitta, 117
Pesikta Rabbati, 35, 103, 122
Pessach, 19, 37, 123
Pharaoh, 105
Philo, 127
Philosophy, Jewish, 67, 115, 120, 127, 128, 129, 132, 138, 147
Phylacteries, 45, 47, 51
Pidyon Haben, 49
Pilgrimage, Festivals, 19, 25, 29
Pirke Avot, 122
Pirke de Rav Kahane, 122
Pirke Rabbi Eliezer, 17, 78, 103

Pittsburgh Platform, 143
Pointerhand, Silver, 41
Pope, 134
Portugal, 16
Prayerbook, 45, 113, 131
Prayershawl, 16, 45, 51, 61
Prepared Table, The, 125
Priest, 81
Privilege of the Forefathers, 97
Procession, 31
Progressive Judaism, 141
Prophecy, Classical, 71, 75, 81, 101, 109, 117, 118, 121, 127, 137, 149
Prophet Reading, 39
Proverbs, 55, 56, 87, 90, 95, 98, 107, 119, 127
Psalms, 5, 29, 31, 45, 47, 55, 64, 68, 82, 86, 87, 90, 98, 108, 111, 112, 113, 119
Purim, 37, 120
Purities, Order of, 122, 123

R

Rabbi, 11, 41, 49, 53, 122, 134, 138, 139, 142, 143, 144, 145
Rabbinic, Literature, 75, 122, 124
Rabbinical Assembly of America, The, 138
Rain, 29, 31, 109
Ram s Horn, 11, 13
Rashi, 124
Rattles, 37
Rebbe, Old, 145, 147, 148
Reclined Sitting, 21
Reconstructionism, 139
Reconstructionist Rabbinical College, 139
Redeemer, 75, 81
Redemption, 13, 15, 22, 49, 63, 75, 76, 147
Redemption of the First Born, 49

Reform Movement, 19, 25, 27, 29, 31, 43, 133, 134, 137, 138, 139, 141, 142, 143, 144
Religion, 16, 33, 63, 67, 85, 101, 109, 123, 127, 130, 133, 134, 138, 144, 147
Religious Schools, 27, 144
Remember, 13, 37
Remorse, 89
Repentance, 15, 148
Repetition, 122, 124, 129
Repetition of the Law, 118, 129
Revelation, 13, 71, 75, 81, 105, 118, 127, 128, 130, 131, 143, 144
Righteous Man, 86, 131
Roasted Egg, 21
Rock of Ages, 33
Rock of Strength, 33
Romans, 21, 22, 25, 39
Rosenzweig, Franz, 144
Rosh Chodesh, 3
Rosh Hashanah, 3, 11
Ruth, Book of, 105, 120, 121

S

Saadiah Ben Joseph Gaon, 127, 128
Sabbath, 5, 6, 7, 29, 31, 35, 37, 39, 40, 41, 45, 49, 51, 61, 72, 120, 122, 134, 137, 142, 143
Sabbath Candles, 5
Sabbath of Sabbaths, 16
Sabbath Soul, 5, 7
Sachs, Nelly, 149
Sacrament, 55
Safed, 125
Saltwater, 21
Salvation Army, 147
Samaria, 119
Samaritan Translation of Bible, 117
Samuel, Prophet, 118

Sanctification of the Wine, 5, 21
Sanctuary, 30, 31
Sandek, 49
Sanhedrin, 3
Satan, 85
Saul, King, 118
Save, Please, 29
Sayings of the Fathers, 47, 51, 62, 64, 73, 87, 102, 122
Sayings of Rabbi Natan, 123
Schneerson, Menachem Mendel, Rabbi, 145, 147
School, 41
Schul, 41
S-Chut Avot, 97
Science, 67, 68, 124, 143, 149
Science of Judaism, 137, 143
Scribe, 47
Scullcap, 43
Sea of Talmud, 124
Sedarim, 122
Seder, Celebration, 19, 21, 109
Seeds, 106, 110, 122
Sefer Ha-Kuzari, 128
Sefirat Haomer, 25
Separation, 5
Sephardic Jews, 31
Septuagint, 117
Sermon, 45, 121, 141
Service, 11, 15, 16, 41, 43, 62, 141, 142
Shabbat, Day of Rest, 1
Shacharit, 11, 43
Shaddai, 57
Shaliach Zibbur, 43
Shamash, 33
Shankbone, 21
Shas, 123
Shavuot, 25, 27, 120
Shekalim, 37
Shekel, 37
Shema, The, 43, 45, 57, 61
Shemot, 118
Shimon Bar Jochai, Rabbi, 9, 25
Shimon Ben Lakish, Rabbi, 9
Shir Hashirim, 120
Shivah, 61

Shloshim, 61
Shmini Atzeret, 31
Shmone Essre, 43
Shmuel, Prophet, 118
Shneur Zalman, 145, 147
Shoah, 85
Shochet, 57
Shofar, Blowing of the, 11, 16, 31
Shofarot, 13
Shoftim, 118
Shulchan Aruch, 125, 133
Shushan Purim, 37
Shuv, 15
Shvat, 3
Sichrono Livrachah, 62
Siddur, 45, 113
Sifra, 121
Sifra to Leviticus, 95, 96, 100
Sifre, 121
Sifre to Deuteronomy, 108
Sifre to Ekev, 114
Sifre to Haasinu, 114
Silver Box, 7
Simchat Torah, 31
Simon's Knapsack, 122
Sin, 85, 86, 89, 148
Sinai, Mt., 3, 11, 13, 25, 71, 81, 105, 118
Singer, Isaac, Bashevis, 149
Sivan, 3, 25
Six Orders of the Mishnah, 123
Slaughterer, 57
Solomon Ben Isaac, 124
Solomon, King, 119, 120
Son of the Commandment, 51
Song of Songs, 107, 108, 120, 121, 122, 127
Sorbonne, 147
Soul of Man, 81, 127, 128, 145, 149
Source of Life, The, 128
Soviet Russia, 147
Spain, 16, 39, 113, 124, 128
Spices, 7
Splendor, Book of, 131

Spring Festival, 19
Star of David, 41, 43
Streimel, 149
Strong Hand, The, 124
Study, 49, 123
Sukkah, 29, 31
Sukkot, 3, 29, 109, 120, 148
Sunday, 142
Sura, 127
Symbol in Judaism, 43, 49, 55
Synagogue, 11, 25, 29, 31, 33, 37, 41, 43, 45, 47, 49, 61, 110, 113, 149
Syrian, King, 33
Syrian Translation of Bible, 117

T

Taanit Esther, 39
Tabernacles, Festival of, 29
Tale, The, 19
Tallit, 16, 45, 51, 61
Talmud, 15, 123, 124, 141, 142, 143, 149
Talmud, Bab., Avoda Sara, 65, 87
Talmud, Bab., Baba Batra, 48, 111
Talmud, Bab., Baba Kamma, 102
Talmud, Bab., Baba Metzia, 99
Talmud, Bab., Berachot, 47, 48, 91, 95, 102, 107
Talmud, Bab., Chullin, 83, 87
Talmud, Bab., Eruvin, 114
Talmud, Bab., Gittin, 95, 99
Talmud, Bab., Jebamot, 48, 99
Talmud, Bab., Ketubot, 62, 112
Talmud, Bab., Kiddushin, 98, 99
Talmud, Bab., Maccot, 65
Talmud, Bab., Megillah, 24, 38, 107
Talmud, Bab., Pessachim, 32, 82
Talmud, Bab., Rosh Hashana, 14, 40
Talmud, Bab., Sanhedrin, 77, 78, 83, 87
Talmud, Bab., Shabbat, 9, 28, 35, 62, 65, 91, 99, 114
Talmud, Bab., Sota, 23, 99
Talmud, Bab., Sukkah, 32
Talmud, Bab., Taanit, 38, 40, 48, 77

Talmud, Bab., Yoma, 17, 87, 91, 99
Talmud, Jer. Chagiga, 112
Talmud, Jer. Pea, 59, 99
Talmud, Jer. Pessashim, 24
Talmud, Jer. Rosh Hashana, 14
Talmud, Jer. Shekalim, 87
Talmud, Jer. Taanit, 87
Tammuz, 3, 39
Tanna Debe Elijahu, 96, 100, 108
Tanya, 147
Targum, 117
Teacher's Day, 25
Teachings, In Judaism, 63, 71, 75, 85, 101, 115, 123, 128, 129, 130, 149
Tefillah, 43
Tefillin, 45, 51, 148
Tehillim, 119
Temple, 3, 21, 25, 29, 33, 37, 39, 41, 43, 49, 89, 101, 119, 120, 123, 130
Tenach, 117
Ten Commandments, 11, 27, 105, 118
Ten Days, 11
Teshuvah, 15, 89, 148
Tevet, 3, 39
Theological Seminary, 134
Thirteen Principles, 63, 129
Thomas Acquinas, 129
Thursday, 40, 45
Tiberias, 1
Tishri, 3, 11, 15, 29, 39
Titus, 39
Tohorot, 122, 123
Torah, 11, 25, 31, 49, 51, 97, 117, 121, 122, 127, 128, 130, 131, 143, 145, 147, 148, 149
Torah Feast, 31
Torah Reading, 11, 31, 37, 45, 51
Torah Scroll, 11, 29, 41
Torquemada, 39
Tosefta, 123

Tosefta Berachot, 48
Tossafot, 124
Tractate Sofrim, 51
Tradition, Jewish, 1, 5, 25, 29, 41, 43, 49, 51, 57, 62, 63, 75, 101, 119, 120, 121, 123, 130, 131, 137, 139, 141, 142, 143, 144, 147, 149
Trop, 41
Tzitzit, 45

U

Ufaratztah, 148
Uniqueness of God, 43, 67
Unity of Israel, 101, 144
Universalism, 142, 144
Universities, 147

V

Vajikrah, 118
Venice, Italy, 124
Vision, Sabbath, 39
Vulgata, 117

W

Washing of Hands, 21
Way of Life, Jewish, 1
Week of Mourning, 61
Weekly Portion, Reading of, 31
Western Wall, 39
White Bread, 5
Wiesel, Elie, 150
William of Auvergne, 129
Willow Branches, 29
Wins-Purim, 37
Wise, Isaac Mayer, 143
Wissenschaft des Judentums, 143
Women, Order of, 122
World Union for Progressive Judaism, 144

Y

Yad Ha-Chasakah, 124
Yamin Noraim, 11
Year, Jewish, 1, 15, 149
Yeshiva University, 134
Yiddish, 41, 113, 147
Yom Hadin, 11
Yom Hazikaron, 11
Yom Kippur, 15, 89
Yom Teruah, 11

Z

Zachor, 37
Zaddik, 131, 132
Zecharia, Prophet, 35, 40, 77, 78, 94, 119
Zephania, Prophet, 114, 119
Zeraim, 122
Zichronot, 13
Zion, 39, 53, 75, 109, 110, 141
Zionism, 131, 149
Zohar, Book of, 131

Born in Germany, Professor Kalir studied at the University of Berlin, as well as the Hochschule Fuer die Wissenschaft des Judentums where he was ordained as a Rabbi. Among his teachers were Martin Buber, Leo Baeck, Julius Guttmann, Ch. Albeck, Ismar Elbogen and Hermann Oncken. He received his Ph.D. from one of the oldest European universities, the University of Wuerzburg, Germany.

Professor Kalir was a Rabbi in Germany and Sweden and lived in Israel for sixteen years where he concentrated on the field of higher education and was active in communications and the media. He published books and articles in Hebrew. He was one of the founders of the Radio Broadcasting Station "Kol Zion Lagolah" (Voice of Zion for the Diaspora).

For the past twenty three years, Dr. Kalir has been residing in the United States and teaching at Brooklyn College, New York, Hebrew College in Boston, Massachusetts, and for the last ten years at the California State University at Fullerton, California.

Being a distinguished scholar in his field, Professor Kalir has appeared on national television and publishes regularly in magazines and periodicals covering a wide range of religious topics.

This is his fifth book.

LIBRARY OF DAVIDSON COLLEGE